THE COMPLETE GUIDE TO REAL ESTATE MARKETING

DIEGO DE GIOVANNI

DEDICATION

I want to dedicate this book to all the people who have supported me by my side and encouraged me in these twenty years of experience.
And then of course as always the biggest dedication goes to my family, my partner Alessia and my daughter Alice.

Table of Contents

Introduction 1
Categories of Real Estate 2
  Residential Real Estate... 2
  Commercial Real Estate.. 4
  Industrial Real Estate... 5
  LAND.. 6
Real Estate Industry.. 7
Real Estate Investing... 9
  Tips for proper Investment... 12
    Location... 12
    Real Estate Agent 13
    Choosing the best loan.. 14
    Types of property... 14
How to Profit from Real Estate................................... 17
  Appreciation.. 17
  Income 18
Home Statistics in Relation to Real Estate 20
Real Estate Wholesaling.. 23
  The Idea... 23
  How It Operates... 24
  The Benefits of Wholesale Investing in Real Estate....... 25
    The Legal Debates 25
Being A Real Estate Agent... 29
  Tips to Become a Good Real Estate Agent 29
    Real estate is a small business 29
    Leads and listings, yet not necessarily in that order......... 32
    Relationships are everything..................................... 34
    Develop a personality. 37

Things to do before Starting a Real Estate Career . 39

Be Honest with Yourself. 39

Interview Current Real Estate Professionals. 40

Know how exactly to Budget and take action. 41

Consider a Second Source of Income 42

Start Building your Database of Contacts.....................42

Treat this as a small business (since it is!)......................43

Learn through the Best...43

Research the greatest Broker Firm for you. 44

Arrive at Know your Neighborhood and Surrounding

Area. 45

Get Licensed. 45

Starting a real Estate Business 46

Planning 46

Market research and idea validation..............................47

Do general market trends early 48

Do market research to assess your personal skills.........48

Get some good real-world experience or find a mentor .49

Branding 51

Making it legal...54

Getting financed 56

Setting up shop 58

Marketing and launching 60

Career in Real Estate 62

Employed by Yourself..62

Finding a brokerage..64

The "Split" 66

How Much Cash Can You Make? 67

What you ought to Get Going 68

Real Estate License: 68

MLS Access: 69

Board of Realtor Dues:..69

Computer:...69

Smart Phone: 69

Car: 70

Business Cards: 70

Signage: 70

Clothing: 71

Get Going! 71

Real Estate Commission Rates 72

Where Does the Money Go? 72

Buyer & Seller Agent Splits 73

Brokerage Splits 73

Agent Costs 73

It's Exactly About the Web 75

Commission Rates Are Negotiable 76

Bonuses & Incentives 77

Real estate commission rates 77

Is career as a Real Estate Agent Right for you 78

Education Requirements Can Be Minimal 79

The Cash Is Great, Eventually 80

You'll Enjoy Flexible Hours, Sometimes 81

You're Helping People 82

The Tech Advantage 82

The professionals of a Real Estate Career 83

The Cons of a vocation in Real Estate 83

Real Estate Careers For those who don't want to buy and sell Homes 86

Commercial Real Estate Salesperson 86

Real Estate Broker 87

Business Broker 88

Loan Officer 88

Home Inspector 89

Real Estate Appraiser 90

Real Estate Assistant 90

Real Estate Developer 91

House Flipper 91

Landlord or Property Manager 92

How to Finance Your Real Estate Business 93

   Hard Money Lender 93

   Microloans 94

   Real Estate Crowdfunding 94

   SBA Loans 95

   ROBS..96

Real Estate and Artificial Intelligence...................... 98

   Artificial intelligence will alter the real estate industry:99

      Data Management: 99

      Getting Data-Driven Insights: 99

      Property Price Calculations:............................100

      Lead Management:..100

      Customers Interaction: 101

      Reduces the cost of real estate services:..........101

      Helps in the commercial transaction: 101

   How will artificial intelligence in real estate work 101

      Two phrases: Lease Abstraction.......................101

   What does the industry think? 103

Real Estate Marketing 106

   Market Yourself 106

   Offer Home Valuations to fully capture Seller Leads ..106

   Leverage Influencer Marketing 107

   Generate Referrals by Hosting Community Events.....107

   Make Your Website Your Storefront...............108

   Create Real Estate Websites............................108

   Provide a Complimentary Moving Truck.....................109

   Use Instagram Stories 109

   Send Postcards..110

   Optimize Your Facebook Page........................110

   Create Subdivision Website Pages...................111

   Highlight Homes With Professional Photography 111

   Use Unique Décor to Set Your Listing Apart 112

   Live Stream Your Agency's Day-to-Day.......................112

   Choose Words That Sell 113

Focus Your Marketing Efforts 113

Make Connections with Local Businesses 114

Showcase Your Charitable Side 114

Create a Blog That Answers Client Questions 115

Create a Video Series to generally share With Leads .. 115

Stick Out with Handwritten Notes 116

Google Ads 116

Increase Your Network 117

Target Serious Leads 117

Make your own Reference to Video Emails 118

Host an Annual Party for Clients 118

Harness the ability of Cold Calling 119

Use Strategic PR to construct Authority 120

Craft a Personalized Message for Your Buyers 120

Suit your message to your seller 121

Use Retargeting Campaigns to Drive Website Traffic 121

Host Local Neighborhood Tours 121

Choose the Right Farm Area 122

Start an immediate Marketing Campaign 122

Write a Killer Real Estate Newsletter 123

Create a New & Eye-catching Logo 123

Master Your Elevator Pitch 124

Use SEO to push Traffic to Your Website 124

Create a Client Testimonial Packet 125

Create Viral Infographics to fairly share on Social Media
.... 125

Share a Viral Real Estate Video 125

Some More Outside-the-Box Real Estate Marketing
Ideas 127

Build a Rock Solid Marketing Foundation 128

Publish a nearby market quiz on the real estate website
.... 129

Offer Home Valuations to Capture Seller Leads 130

Valuation report 130

Provide a no cost moving truck.............................131
Answer buyer/seller questions in your blog.................132
Add some flavor to your real estate video marketing. .133
Develop a blog post or video series highlighting great
area restaurants and entertainment 134
Order unique business cards that stick out..................135
Incorporate your furry friend into several of your real
estate listing photos 136
Use Instagram Stories 137
Devise a fun game to accompany awards shows or
televised events 138
Post ideas and strategies for homeowners, buyers, and
sellers in Reddit. 138
Capitalize on the rise in popularity of the latest internet
memes...139
Fabricate mock logos for your agency that replicate
famous ones..140
Send Handwritten Notes......................................140
Create a referral system 141
Real Estate Marketing Niches..............................141
Real Estate Branding Ideas 142
Develop a value proposition..............................143
Acquire some swag printed with your branding............144
Ask your best former clients for testimonials.................144
Have an original signature item or look. 145
Set up squeeze pages or lead capture forms on your own
site for lead gen. 145
Place your contact information on every page of your
website...145
Include beautiful royalty-free local imagery. 146
Give leads expense information and calculators. 146
Use calls to action to boost user engagement. 146
Add testimonials to your homepage. 147
Add social sharing buttons to your site. 147

Write and publish content on the blog regularly. 147

Develop guides for buyers and sellers. 148

Vary post types. 148

Use analytics to operate a vehicle your marketing......... 149

Real Estate Listing Marketing Ideas.............................. 149

Optimize listing pages. 149

Feature top listings from the home page 149

Construct great real estate listing copy. 150

Make your listings look their best................................... 150

Dedicate blog posts or landing pages to showcase your listings at length. 150

Advertise listings in a separate newsletter to your leads and clients... 151

Create video presentations for your listings................... 151

Post listing all about every social networking outlet. 151

Develop listing boards on Pinterest. 152

Real Estate Social Media Marketing Ideas................... 152

Social media marketing 152

Create custom social media bios for every single platform. 153

Invite relatives and buddies to such as your pages or follow you. 153

Post regularly on each social media marketing platform. 154

Include social follow buttons on your own website. 155

Showcase your savvy with video................................... 155

Get a social media scheduler. 155

Join a Twitter discussion.. 156

Run a contest through social networking. 157

Publish new, original thoughtful articles on LinkedIn... 157

Discover ways to set up advertising campaigns............. 157

Choose a vendor to setup campaigns for you. 158

Creating an ad budget. 158

Use social media marketing. 159

Develop captivating graphics for ads. 159

Advertise in high-audience newsletters. 159

Create a dedicated splash page attached to your ad........159

Create custom media around featured properties. 160

Targeted video advertising of single properties..............160

Layer on retargeting across key channels.......................160

Real Estate SEO **160**

Put up a Google My Business page................................160

LA RE agents 161

Submit site to major aggregators....................................161

Ensure consistent NAP across all online properties 162

Set up schema...163

Conduct key word research 163

Build local landing pages 165

Collect reviews on major 3rd party review sites 165

Local search factors..166

Build local backlinks 166

Monitor backlinks 166

Real Estate Email Marketing Ideas 166

Offline Real Estate Marketing Ideas **169**

Sponsor local events. 170

Host free seminars on topics concerning buyers or sellers
in your area...170

Advertise your company and listings in local media.......170

Take local sponsorships one step further.........................170

Run an open house. 171

Use custom banners, balloons, and signs to market your
open house...171

Create a physical high-quality mailer. 171

Write a consistent column for the local media. 171

Attend local events and join local meetup groups and
associations. 172

Real Estate Video Promotion Tips and Ideas **172**

Interview happy customers...172

Shoot video tours of most listings.................................. 173

Publish home/buyer educational videos......................... 173

Record neighborhood community videos 174

Promote helpful how-to videos...................................... 174

Add videos to email drip series...................................... 175

Promote videos across social media channels............... 175

How to Build a fruitful Real Estate Marketing

Campaign **176**

Set clear goals.. **176**

Identify your target customer...................................... **176**

Establish your unique selling proposition **177**

Choose marketing channels to reach audience **178**

Define a lead nurturing strategy................................... **178**

Select tools to make usage of the plan **179**

Measure performance **179**

Ready. Set. Market. **179**

Buyer's Agent vs. Listing Agent **181**

Fixed Rate vs. Adjustable Rate Mortgages................... **181**

Pre-approval Letter.. **181**

Listings **182**

Inspection **182**

Appraisal **182**

Contingencies **183**

Offers and Contracts... **183**

Closing Costs **184**

Title Insurance **184**

ABOUT THE AUTHOR... **185**

Introduction

Real estate is the property, land, buildings, air rights above the land and underground rights underneath including uncultivated flora and fauna, farmed crops and livestock, water and mineral deposits.The expression real estate means real, or physical, property. "Real" comes from the Latin root res, or things. Others say it is from the Latin word rex, meaning "royal," since kings used to own all land inside their kingdoms.

Real estate is a tangible asset and a form of real property. Real property includes land, buildings as well as other improvements, in addition to the rights of good use and enjoyment of that land and all sorts of its improvements. Renters and leaseholders might have rights to inhabit land or buildings that are considered an integral part of their estate, but these rights themselves are not, strictly speaking, considered real estate.

Real property is not the same as and may not to ever be mistaken for personal property. Personal property includes intangible assets like investments, along with tangible assets such as for example furniture and fixtures like a dishwasher. Also, even renters may claim areas of a property as personal property, provided you bought and installed the property using the lessor's permission.

Categories of Real Estate

Real estate have different categories which we have looked into in this book, the categories include;

- Residential Real Estate
- Commercial Real Estate
- Industrial Real Estate
- Land

Residential Real Estate

Residential real estate includes undeveloped land, houses, condominiums, and town houses. The structures might be single-family or multi-family dwellings and could be owner occupied or rental properties.

Within the 2019 edition of its annual home-value analysis, the real estate website Zillow estimated the full total worth of all U.S. homes in 2018 was $33.3 trillion, 71% more than the country's gross domestic product (GDP) of $19.4 trillion at that time. Homeownership, also called owner-occupancy, is one of common type's of real estate investment in america. In line with the National Multifamily Housing Council (NMHC), roughly two-thirds of residents own their home. Often, these owners have financed the acquisition by taking out a mortgage loan, when the property will act as collateral when it comes to debt.

Individuals shopping for home mortgages to assist them to realize the dream of property ownership are faced with many different options. Mortgages can charge either fixed-rate or variable-rate interest. Fixed-rate mortgages generally have higher interest rates than variable-rate mortgages, which could make them higher priced within the short run. Fixed-rate loans cost more for the short term as they are protected from future rate of interest increases.

Banks publish amortization schedules that show simply how much of a borrower's monthly obligations head to paying off interest versus how much goes to paying down the principal of the loan. Balloon loans are mortgages that do not fully amortize reduce to zero over time. Instead, the borrower pays interest for a group period, 5 years as an example, and then must pay the remaining associated with loan in a balloon payment at the end of the expression.

Also, mortgages go along with heavy costs that include transaction fees and taxes. These additional expenses in many cases are rolled in to the loan.

Once potential homeowners' have proven their eligibility and secured a mortgage from a bank or any other lender, they have to complete additional steps to make sure the property is legally on the market plus in good shape.

Residential Real Estate also Includes both new construction and resale homes. The most common category is single-family homes. There are condominiums, co-ops, townhouses, duplexes, triple-deckers, quadplexes, high-value homes, multi-generational and vacation homes.

Commercial Real Estate

Commercial real estate includes non residential structures such as for instance office buildings, warehouses, and retail buildings. These buildings could be free standing or in shopping malls.

Commercial real estate is used for commerce and includes anything from strip malls and free standing restaurants to office buildings and skyscrapers. It is often distinguished from industrial real estate, which is practical space utilized in the manufacturing of products.

Buying or leasing real estate for commercial purposes is extremely not the same as buying a house or even buying residential real estate.

Commercial leases are generally longer than residential leases. Commercial real estate returns are derived from their profitability per square foot, unlike structures intended to be private residences. Moreover, lenders may necessitate a more substantial down payment on home financing for commercial real estate then what exactly is needed for a residence.

Commercial real estate also Includes shopping malls and strip malls, medical and educational buildings, hotels and offices. Apartment buildings in many cases are considered commercial, even though they've been utilized for residences. Which is since they are owned to produce income.

Industrial Real Estate

Industrial real estate includes factories, business parks, mines, and farms. These properties usually are larger in size and locations can include access to transportation hubs such as for instance rail lines and harbors.

This includes manufacturing buildings and property, as well as warehouses. The buildings may be used for research, production, storage and distribution of products. Some buildings that distribute goods are considered commercial real estate. The classification is important due to the fact zoning, construction and sales are handled differently.

LAND

Includes land that is vacant working farms and ranches. The subcategories within vacant land include undeveloped, early development or reuse, subdivision and site assembly.

Real Estate Industry

Real estate also relates to producing, buying and selling real estate. Real estate affects the U.S. economy when you're a crucial driver of economic growth.

Construction of brand new buildings is an element of gross domestic product. It offers both residential, commercial, and industrial buildings. In 2018, real estate construction contributed $1.15 trillion to the nation's economic output. That is 6.2 percent of U.S. gross domestic product. It is more than the $1.13 trillion in 2017, but nevertheless not as much as the 2006 peak of $1.19 trillion. During those times, real estate construction was a hefty 8.9 percent element of GDP.

New house building is a critical category. It offers construction of single-family homes, town houses and condominiums. The National Association of Home Builders provides monthly data on home sales and average prices. The info on new house sales is a leading economic indicator. It signals the way the housing industry can do in nine months. That's how long it will require to construct new homes. The NAHB also reports new home starts, those would be the quantity of home construction projects on which ground is broken.

Real estate professionals assist homeowners, businesses and investors buy and sell all four types of properties. The industry is usually divided up into specialists that focus using one of this types.

Sellers' agents help find buyers through either the Multiple Listing Service or their professional contacts. They price your premises, using comparative listings of recently sold properties known as "comps". The will allow you to spruce up your property therefore it can look its best to customers. They help in negotiations using the buyer, assisting you to get the highest price possible. Listed here are more sellers' agent services.

Buyers' agents provide similar services for the home purchaser. They know the local market. That means they are able to find a property that meets your most significant criteria. Additionally they compare prices, called "doing comps." It allows them to guide you to areas that are affordable. Buyers' agents negotiate for you personally, pointing out reasons why the vendor should accept a lower life expectancy price. They assistance with the legalities for the process, including title search, inspection and financing.

Real Estate Investing

Everyone who buys or sells a property engages in real estate investing. This means you have to consider several factors. Will the home increase in value whilst you live in it? If you get a home loan, how will future interest rates and taxes affect you?

Many individuals do this well with investing within their homes they wish to buy and sell homes as a business. There are numerous methods to accomplish that. First, you can easily flip a home. That's where you get a home to enhance then sell it. Lots of people own several homes and rent them out. Others use Airbnb as a convenient way to rent out all or section of their homes. It is possible to rent vacation homes using VRBO or Home Away.

You are able to invest in housing without buying a house. You should buy stocks of homebuilders. Their stock prices rise and fall with all the housing industry. Another way is by using Real Estate Investment Trusts, called REITS. They are investments in commercial real estate. Their stock prices lag behind trends in residential real estate by a few years.

Unlike other investments, real estate is dramatically affected by its surroundings and immediate geographic area. Hence the well-known real-estate maxim "location, location, location." Except for a severe national recession or depression, residential real estate values, in particular, are affected primarily by local factors. Such factors include the area's employment rate, the area economy, crime rates, transportation facilities, quality of schools, municipal services, and property taxes.

You will find key variations in residential and commercial real estate investments. From the one hand, residential real estate is generally less costly and smaller than commercial real estate, and so it is more affordable for the small investor.

On the other hand, commercial real estate is often times more valuable per sq ft, and its leases are longer, which theoretically ensures a far more predictable income stream. With greater revenue comes greater responsibility. Commercial rental real estate is more heavily regulated than residential real estate, and these regulations may vary not merely from nation to nation and state by state but additionally by county and city. Even within cities, zoning regulations add a layer of unwanted complexity to commercial real estate investments.

There is increased risk of tenant turnover in commercial rental agreements. In the event that lessee's business design is bad, their product is unattractive, or they truly are poor managers, they might file for bankruptcy. The business failure can abruptly stop expensive real estate from generating revenue.

Moreover, just like property can appreciate, it can also depreciate. Once-hot retail locations have been proven to decay into rotten shopping malls and dead malls.

Pros

• Offers steady income

• Offers capital appreciation

• Diversifies portfolio

• Can be bought with leverage

Cons

• Is usually illiquid

• Influenced by highly local factors

• Requires big initial capital outlay

• May require active management, expertise

Tips for proper Investment

Many people has jump into the property investment bandwagon. In the past, buying a property for the true purpose of selling in a nutshell term was definitely tempting and possible. To date, buying a residential property and selling it in a short time is definitely harder as compared to decades ago. Simply because the house market has slowed down significantly and property prices no longer rise as much as a result of government's measure to cool off the market.

Location

First of all, do keep in mind location plays a crucial role with regards to property investment. The positioning you like will have an effect on the price plus the potential growth in the near future.

How do you define "good location"? Look at the location of the property. May be the property located at a spot that is ideal to live in? Is the location convenient? Does the area have easy option of public transport and amenities? Are there any public transportations such as train station nearby? What are the education institutions within the vicinities? These are all the factors which will affect and determine the buying price of the property and the rental yield.

On a side note, you should stay close to your home investment if you intend to rent it out. This will save you from plenty of hassle when it comes to handling tenant complaints and maintenance.

Real Estate Agent

Finding the right real estate agent is essential as well. A beneficial real estate agent could save you from hassles and stress as they begin to be the anyone to handle any property related matters on your behalf. All things considered, they truly are real estate professionals with professional expertise that you don't have. Furthermore, they definitely have significantly more experience than you are doing when it comes to handling property related matters.

If you're looking for the best property to buy, tell your real estate agent according to your preferences and they will perform some rest to find you an ideal property with favorable price. If you should be about to rent out your home, they're going to then enable you to seek out potential tenants. With all the right real estate agent, it is possible to definitely sell out or rent out your home much easier and far quicker.

Choosing the best loan

Once we know that properties fit in with illiquid assets, it may never be a great idea to place all your valuable money in properties. You will need to understand that the entire process of selling a house just isn't easy. It might take approximate 6 months to a year, or more to sell off the property. Even so, the purchase price that you will be selling the house is probably not the best price. Hence, it is advisable to opt for a home loan to finance your investment. With so many loans offered by different banks, it is crucial for you yourself to educate yourself on the loans available. Find out of the difference between interest levels, prepayment penalties and settlement cost offered by different banks. Make sure you choose the loan that best you prefer.

In addition, you are able to make use of the money you can get from your own rental income to fund your monthly mortgage instalments. In order to make a profit from renting out your property, the ideal instalment is approximately 60% for the rental income you receive.

Types of property

There are lots of types of property available, such as for example condominiums, apartments and landed properties. You will need to select the right variety of property according to your requirements. Landed properties are often more costly than condominium units or apartment units. However, landed properties appreciate more in value in comparison with apartments. That said, you need to invest in landed property, even just one storey house is going to do, because it will provide you with more advantages ultimately.

This however does not mean apartments are not a worthy investment. Apartments or condominiums are more suited to renting. In addition, it really is more appealing to very first time property buyers due to the fact price is relatively cheaper than landed properties. Be sure you always stay within your budget.

Last but most certainly not least, do take into account on the types of property you spend money on, in terms of leasehold property or freehold property. Leasehold property has a limited leasing period (normally 99 years) which is renewable. As for freehold property, it really is a residential property with no leasing period. This means, the house is yours forever.

property investment isn't as difficult because it seems. It might appear daunting but the return is definitely worth the time and effort and money which you have call at, provided you made it happen the right way. Make sure you research your facts and plan ahead before buying properties for investment purpose to avoid getting into financial debts. All things considered, it really is an investment that costs a lot and does not come cheap.

How to Profit from Real Estate

One could invest in real estate directly by purchasing actual properties or parcels of land; or indirectly, by buying shares in publicly traded real estate investment trusts (REITs) or mortgage-backed securities (MBS). The indirect investment methods may offer less return and less control, but they are vastly more liquid than owning physical real estate and don't require in-depth familiarity with the real estate business.

Investing directly in real estate leads to profits or losses through two avenues, which may haven't changed in centuries:

- Revenue from rent or leases
- Appreciation associated with real estate's value

Appreciation

Appreciation is achieved through different means, but the boost in a property's value isn't realized until the owner sells his house. Another way to comprehend profit is to refinance the mortgage. Raw and undeveloped land, like the territory right outside a city's borders, supplies the biggest potential for construction, enhancement, and profit. Appreciation can also result from discovering valuable materials or natural resources on a plot of land, like striking oil. Also, an increase in the market values of the area all over land you possess.

As a neighborhood grows and develops, property values have a tendency to climb. The gentrification of urban neighborhoods in some American cities during the last few decades has often led to a dramatic increase in real estate prices. Scarcity also can may play a role in the worth of real estate holdings. If a whole lot is the last of the size or kind in a prestigious area or one where such lots rarely become available it gains in marketability.

Income

Income from real estate comes in many forms. The greatest generator may be the rent paid on land already progressed into residential or commercial properties. However, companies will even pay royalties for natural resource discoveries on raw land. Also, they could pay to build structures upon it, like cell towers or pipelines.

Income can also come from indirect real estate investments. In a REIT, the owner of multiple properties sells shares to investors and passes along rental income by means of distributions. Similarly, in an MBS, the interest and principal payments from a pool of mortgages are collected and passed through to investors.

Both REITs and MBS investment products trade like stocks, with real estate acting as their underlying security. So, they could offer capital appreciation could be the shares gain in market value.

Home Statistics in Relation to Real Estate

Statistics about new home construction are important leading economic indicators. This means they are going to give you an advance notice on the future associated with housing market.

All these indicators tells just a little different story concerning the health for the homebuilding industry. For instance, say home starts are steady, but housing starts decline. That will take a toll on home sales. Many buyers might not desire to wait more than a year. Moreover it means there's a shortage of lumber, concrete, or construction workers. Those shortages could drive up costs, and sales prices. That could further decrease need for new homes.

If mortgages are declining, the homebuilder will end up with a listing of unsold homes for sale. In addition it means demand is high, but homeowners can not get mortgages. Rising home starts may appear like an indication of housing strength. But it may be a negative sign. Declining home closings mean the housing market is weak.

The brand new home sale is the initial step in a nine to twelve-month process. If new house sales pick up, then you definitely know closings will boost in about a year. However, all of the remaining three steps should be completed.

A fresh home sales occurs when the buyer signs the paperwork and provides the homebuilder a deposit. That's since most new homes are not constructed until there is a buyer. The exceptions are spec homes which can be used as model homes. The Census Bureau releases monthly estimates of the latest home sales. They are given as an annual rate.

2 months following the paperwork is signed, your local housing regulators grant the permit. It is an early on indicator, not always accurate. Builders can go bankrupt and do not build the permitted units. They could replace the number of units built in a multi-family. In fact, 22.5 percent of multi-family permits aren't built, or are changed to single-family units. Finally, developers often receive permits for a large percentage of a complex that could take months and month to build.

90 days later is the new house start. It occurs when the builder breaks ground. The National Association of Home Builders reports with this

monthly. It's very accurate since the new home start only takes place when the builder is confident enough to break ground.

Six to nine months later could be the closing. The homebuyer must receive home financing before the home can close. If the homebuyer does not qualify, your house remains in inventory. If this statistic is lower than the home sale figure, it means this new real estate market will quickly slow down. There are too many homes being built, rather than enough qualified home buyers. It may also mean builders will begin lowering prices to clear their inventories. Fannie Mae releases the report on all mortgages.

You will find three other important indicators to view.

Inventory - This is the total of homes that are offered for sale, but unsold. The NAHB reports this monthly.

Months of Supply this is one way many months it can decide to try sell all the houses in inventory. It is on the basis of the sales rate and inventory. The NAHB also reports this monthly.

Sales Prices - The Census Bureau reports on both the median and average new house sales price.

Real Estate Wholesaling

Real estate wholesaling generally seems to be growing in visibility. How exactly does it work?

Flipping houses happens to be ever more popular in modern times. Wholesaling is a form of house flipping, and may even prove to be a key strategy more investors will embrace into the developing housing market. So, so how exactly does it work? Exactly what are the benefits? What role might real estate agents play in the process?

The Idea

Many people have trouble with new concepts like wholesaling real estate, however the basic idea has been a typical section of our economy and shopping habits for a long time. Probably the most notable examples of this are Walmart, Costco, and Amazon.

Walmart has generated a huge footprint on its ability to buy inventory in large volume at affordable prices and sell that inventory at a profit. It's businesses like these and their logistics which have also helped legendary investors like Warren Buffett get to be the richest people on earth.

Grocery and consumer goods wholesaler Costco is continuing to grow even bigger than Walmart in certain areas, grossing almost $120B a year ago. Amazon has established a digital platform which essentially wholesales almost everything you can ever are interested to buy.

How It Operates

Real estate wholesaling works much like any other kind of wholesaling. The theory is to purchase properties low, and sell for a profit to another end buyer. Most commonly, this is done by targeting discounted or undervalued properties, and then flipping them to rehabbers or rental property investors. Some wholesalers flip their properties to regular retail buyers, others focus on bulk portfolio deals.

Some wholesalers buy and sell properties for cash. Others use short term financing like credit lines, hard money, or transactional funding. Others concentrate on simply securing and assigning, or 'flipping' contracts.

Wholesaling real estate differs from traditional fixing and flipping of houses in that these investors generally don't do any rehab work. They purchase and sell as-is. Though some may do minor cleaning up, make cosmetic improvements, or 'prehab' to create on a clean slate for the next buyer.

The Benefits of Wholesale Investing in Real Estate

Among the list of top reasons investors choose this owning a home strategy include:

- One of the easiest real estate strategies to master
- Speed of getting in, out, and paid
- No handyman or construction experience needed
- Short holdings times which reduce risk and costs
- High profit margins
- Can work in up and down markets

The Legal Debates

There are often debates about the legality of flipping and wholesaling houses. Some argue that wholesaling is illegal. Often that is because of misconceptions concerning the strategy. Various other cases it is a matter of not conducting activities which require a license, in the event that you don't get one. It's important that all individual do their research, know their local laws, and consult legal counsel and licensed professionals for guidance. Make certain you stick to the law and wholesaling isn't only legal, but highly profitable as well.

House Flipping Statistics

RealtyTrac tracks homes which are bought and sold within 12 months, and so are considered flips. Wholesale properties certainly are categorized as this category. To demonstrate the possibility for this strategy the latest stats through the annual House Flipping Report show the following:

- 193,009 houses were flipped this past year
- Almost 6% of all house and condo sales just last year were flips
- 126,256 individuals and business entities flipped houses this past year
- The typical house flipping gross profit in 2016 was $62,624
- More than 11 cities have average profits of over $100,000
- The average ROI is 49.2%
- 9 cities posted flipping profits above 75% just last year
- Wholesaling MLS Properties

You'll find so many methods to find wholesale property deals. Including:

- Newspaper ads
- Craigslist
- Foreclosure auctions
- Bank REOs
- Your very own website
- Social media marketing
- The MLS

Some real estate trainers focus on more guerrilla marketing methods of finding deals. Others find they can build a fantastic pipeline of business from Realtors and properties on the Multiple Listing Service. This might save time and costs, and make certain consistency in volume, while benefiting from the legal protection of employing an authorized agent. Built with the right information, good negotiation skills, in accordance with some remarketing help investors can leverage the incredible number of properties into the MLS and from the other sources, to construct a proper business that has the potential for making millions of dollars a year.

Find a real estate agent familiar with Real Estate Wholesaling on UpNest!

The numbers recorded by RealtyTrac plus the popularity of top wholesaling brands suggest this could be a profitable strategy for others. There are clear advantages of wholesaling for people who are simply getting started, with a great amount of growth and long term potential as well. There are a variety of ways to get started, including reaching out to local real estate agents for help negotiating MLS properties, which could also help investors stick to just the right region of the law. Use UpNest for connecting with top agents in your area, and begin growing your income with real estate wholesaling today!

Being A Real Estate Agent

The actual estate agent could be the workhorse associated with industry. He's a salesman one moment, a buyer's advocate the following; he's an analyst, an auctioneer, a consultant, a negotiator, and a marketer; he occasionally performs the services of an appraiser, a clerk, and a loan officer; he accommodates his clients on nights and weekends, and frequently works well beyond forty hours per week.

Basically, a real estate agent does a little of everything, as well as for that, he's paid a modest commission (provided, of course, that he closes the offer). It's no wonder, then, that a lot of agents cycle inside and outside associated with the industry. It's also no wonder that demand for their services remains high even yet in a slow market.

Tips to Become a Good Real Estate Agent

Real estate is a small business

In recent years we've seen some new trends when it comes to the consumer's relationship with the realtor industry. A lot more than ever before, the typical average person has access to the kinds of statistics, market analyses, technology, and expert opinions which were previously reserved for people who actively made their living as an agent or broker.

Prior to the Internet, a lot of these records would only exist within the mouths of working agents or in agent licensure textbooks. Consumers had little importance of these records simply because they trusted their real estate professional to learn it.

Today, Realtors are blabbing throughout the blogosphere, even making a buck by telling consumers simple tips to do their jobs. "How to generate income in Real Estate: Five Easy Steps." "Flipping Homes for Fun and Profit." Consequently, some appear to think about becoming a realtor like using up an interest, something to occupy your recovery time and get you quick cash at exactly the same time.

But the majority hobbies are cheap, and also the expensive ones are about the sheer enjoyment associated with the activity. With a hobby, you're allowed to be careless since you don't have anything to get rid of. Neglect your herb garden for a couple days? No big deal. Don't play your guitar per month? It'll still be there whenever your fingers obtain the itch.

Real estate, on the other hand, is a small business. It's about money, so when the marketplace has revealed in the last several years, when you are getting careless in real estate, you stand to reduce plenty of it. As a real estate agent, you're an independent contractor, which means it's up to you to manage your own business. Any agent who picks up your slack isn't handing it back once again to you.

Finally, hobbies are personal, while real estate is professional. Typically, only the individuals with whom you decide to share your hobbies know about them, which means they don't have a massive effect on your public image.

But since your conduct as a real estate agent takes place when you look at the professional world, it has much an extended paper trail. Just about anybody can know about it. Fail to satisfy a customer, and you're telling her and everybody she knows that you're unreliable—which may have serious ramifications for other regions of your life.

None for this means you ought ton't enjoy being employed as a Realtor. Quite the opposite, you're not likely to reach your goals in the event that you don't. Nevertheless the best agents are those who marry the pleasure they get from their work to a knowledge that it's, well, work.

Leads and listings, yet not necessarily in that order

It doesn't matter what business you're in, selling is hard. As an agent, however, the challenge is even greater because repeat customers are few and far in between.

Homes, most likely, are not electronics or fashion items. They're not built to be replaced after a year, nor do they become obsolete. People buy homes with the intention of staying put. In a perfect world, your clients won't need you again for a long time.

True, unforeseen circumstances require visitors to move, and based on the latest census, 69.3 percent of most movers stayed within the same county, which means significantly more than two-thirds of movers might be returning to the same Realtor. Nevertheless, altogether only 12.5 percent of the U.S. population changed residences this season. That's a small increase since 2008, but in general, this share has decreased by about 50 % because the late 1940s.

Furthermore, these statistics vary widely depending on where you live. About 14.7 percent of Westerners moved in 2010, but that does you no good in the event that you operate in the Northeast, where only 8.3 percent did exactly the same.

So how do you grow your organization when interest in the services you provide is bound? By working both sides associated with the real estate equation. Several years ago, agents worked exclusively with sellers, listing their properties for sale and rent. In those days, your task would be to have the word out about a seller's property and attract buyers. The more listings you had, the higher off you had been.

Today, however, it's also common to work with the buyer. In this scenario, success is all about leads, folks who are thinking about buying a home. As soon as you've found a lead, your job is always to turn him from a prospect to a customer by helping him secure the house he'd prefer to rent or purchase.

This usually means you're a matchmaker, connecting buyers with listings your agency already has. You might like to be an advocate, helping them browse someone else's listings. In either case, the arrangement is simply exactly the same: agents use their experience to ensure buyers don't get screwed. In the place of selling a property, you're selling your expertise.

So which can be more important, leads or listings? That will depend on where you are. But whatever the figures, it's vital to keep a close eye on both. In an arduous market and a changing industry, the best way to success for an agent is to be adaptable and prepared to work with sellers and buyers. Concentrate solely on a single, and you'll find yourself struggling maintain your business afloat.

Relationships are everything

Every agent is glued to his iPhone or laptop screen these days. However, it is important to remember on the reverse side of all those zeroes and ones are real people, and they're the ones who keep your business going.

Relationships are your bread and butter and when we say that, we're not talking the little dinner rolls you fill up on before your meal arrives.

To know simple tips to maximize your relationships as a realtor, start by asking the basic questions: that do you realize, and that knows you? The answers will go far in revealing the extent of one's sphere of influence, the collection of people for whom you as well as your business have weight. The more your sphere of influence, the greater amount of of a magnet you then become for prospects and the better your chances of turning them into customers.

The cliché goes that real estate is about location. That isn't pretty much inventory: it's about involvement. To optimize your online business, you need to participate in your community. Join your local Realtor's association. Coach just a little league team. Attend town government meetings. Get exposure within the flesh, and make sure people know what you do.

By showing you're enthusiastic about the life span of one's community, you demonstrate that you have an individual stake in every the business enterprise you are doing as a real estate agent. You should also treat everyone you meet up with the same courtesy and attention, no matter who they are or what they can perform for you personally after all, you will never know who may become a person.

Knowing and being known by as many folks that you can is essential, specially when there aren't lots of prospects to go around. But while quantity is great, quality is even better. Visibility is great, but if your only goal is to obtain everyone and anyone from the hook, knowing everybody in the city will really work against you. Your reputation in your community greatly influences your trade. People obviously want to work with agents they trust.

The essential sustainable business design is just one by which your transactions with other people are often mutually beneficial. Real estate, is approximately earning profits; but focus too much on your profit margins, and you'll find you've got fewer and fewer customers looking to hand theirs over.

Finally, as soon as you've established your relationships, it's imperative to have them up, whether or not they're causing you to money right now. Follow through with recent customers to see how they're settling in. Distribute a message newsletter to all your clients. Send personalized notes and birthday cards. Use social media marketing and continue maintaining a presence online. If you feel as you haven't spoken to a vintage customer in a little while, send them a contact to inquire of how they're doing. The gesture only takes one to three minutes, and it will pay huge dividends in the end.

Each contact you make has a value, and every customer has an eternity value. Lose contact with your prospects, leads and customers, and you'll be squandering your greatest asset.

Develop a personality.

It's often said that as a salesman, you're not just selling your product or service: you're selling yourself. That's why as an agent, it's important to develop a personality.

We're not saying you don't get one: we're just suggesting that you lean into it. Whether you're a pet lover, a motorcycle enthusiast, a foodie or an internet gamer, don't hide your personality: embrace it. You're in real estate so, for God's sake, be real. Your personality fosters relationships, which builds your reputation, which generates leads. You will get the picture.

Getting involved in the life of a community helps create your relationships, but it's important that the involvement be in line with who you are as an individual. Enthusiasm is difficult to fake, so if something you say or do doesn't ring true to you personally, individuals will pick up on it.

If you're an enthusiastic carnivore, for instance, shopping for leads at an ASPCA meeting probably is not a beneficial idea and in fact, it might cause both the individuals you meet together with people you are already aware to consider you as a hypocrite.

Instead, you're better off finding opportunities to broadcast yourself to people who have that you have common ground. In terms of those opportunities go, some say it's safer to keep politics and religion out of business, and perhaps those people are right. But politics and religion build strong communities, and according to what your location is, getting involved may have huge benefits. As well, it's important for you to decide what you're comfortable wearing on the sleeve.

We're speaking about work here, therefore it's important to see personality in an expert context. As a whole, moderation and a sense of boundaries are keys to success. Come on too strong or get too personal in your dealings with clients, and you might end up alienating more people than you relate solely to.

Instead, let customers function as the ones to open your responsibility, and they'll often be happier for it after all, many people enjoy speaking about themselves more than anything else.

Things to do before Starting a Real Estate Career

So you're thinking about becoming a realtor? A real estate career is an exciting opportunity that can introduce you to many interesting people and if you work smart can provide a comfortable income. However, there are many things for you yourself to consider and actions to do before beginning the new pursuit.

Here are some the activities to do before launching your real estate career.

Be Honest with Yourself.

This is probably the most important item regarding the list. Essentially, ask yourself (and answer) "what is my motivation?"

If you're driven by the lure of easy money, STOP NOW. It's quite difficult and it also takes a lot of time and effort. The money can come only if you work smart and put forth the time and effort.

If you should be not scared of hard work, enjoy meeting new people and providing a site to others then keep on reading! This can be for your needs.

Real Estate is part marketing, part sales, part entrepreneurship, and a big part customer service. So think through each one of these while making sure you may be willing to do them all, particularly the customer support part.

Will you be good with change? This really is a fast paced business and tools associated with trade are changing rapidly. One minute our company is using laptops and also the next we have been showing homes on tablets. MLS systems are changing quickly as well so we all have to be able to adapt easily to new software and websites. Also, laws are changing and we also must stay as much as date and know the way they impact us and our clients.

Interview Current Real Estate Professionals.

This follows no. 1 very closely. I recommend which you interview several real estate agents to understand the advantages and cons regarding the job. Don't just interview the top agents and/or your real estate professional friends. It is advisable to interview agents at different points inside their career – established agents and ones getting started. Check out questions to think about asking them:

- What exactly are their daily and weekly routines?
- What do they love and hate about their jobs?
- What advice would they give to new agents?
- What do they consider to end up being the most important quality in a great agent?
- What are the common pitfalls to prevent when getting started?
- How important may be the role of technology for the real estate agent?

Once you've your entire questions answered, reflect back in the responses and write a list for the common factors that were mentioned over the interviewees. Arrive at your personal conclusion, and if need be revisit number one on the list to make sure this career is for you.

Know how exactly to Budget and take action.

Taking care of a commission can be very rough for folks who are used to getting regular paychecks. You really must be diligent with your budgeting and savings to avoid adding financial stress on top of the already stressful task of starting an innovative new career. Personal Budgeting is key for longevity as a commissioned sales person.

Consider a Second Source of Income

This may actually serve a couple of purposes.

First, it could relieve financial stress from focusing on commission and never deplete your savings account (and also maybe add to it).

Second, your other job can provide a fantastic source of potential clients and expand your sphere of influence. You should be careful with promoting yourself and new career in excess. Some employer's may frown at this.

Start Building your Database of Contacts

It's never too early to start out compiling a listing of people who you may reach out to and let them know that you're a brand new real estate professional.

Be sure to include as much associated with the following as you can:

- Full Name
- Email
- Home Address

- Home and Mobile Telephone Numbers
- Birth Dates
- List of Family Relations
- Employer and Occupation

Treat this as a small business (since it is!)

When you are getting your real estate license and interviewing agents and firms, you should keep track of your mileage and other expenses. Talk to your tax preparer about allowable expenses and start to trace them accordingly.

Write A Business Strategy. There are several books and resources on the Internet to help with this effort. Planning is extremely important and staying with your plan will assist you to remain on track to earning a profit. Note: you will probably need to modify your first few plans as you receive the hang of the expenses and client conversion ratios so don't be too much on yourself when you have to tweak your plan.

Learn through the Best

There are lots of books and Internet tools offered by top agents that are meant to inspire and teach. The best may be the Millionaire real estate professional by Gary Keller (of Keller Williams). I look at this book when I was initially getting started and can still pick it up whenever I need only a little kick start.

Research the greatest Broker Firm for you.

This can be among the final and vital pieces to possess set up before starting your new career.

You need to try to find a company that has excellent online tools and offers classes and/or mentorships to new agents.

It should be a good fit together with your personality. You will find office politics EVERYWHERE so be sure you are comfortable in your new environment.

Remember through your conversations/ interviews you are interviewing them as well. This is simply not a job interview so do not be nervous. As a realtor you're in business for yourself and you also need to find an excellent partner. The best broker firm could be the partner that will help reach your goals.

Arrive at Know your Neighborhood and Surrounding Area.

It's never prematurily to start looking around, visiting open houses and looking at the costs in your market. Here are a few facts to consider:

- Know the inventory of homes in your selected market.
- Start compiling a list of parks and activities in the region.

Have a go at town meetings and perhaps serve on a committee. This is where you are going to hear information first as well as have the ability to expand your contact database.

You are not only selling homes but also neighborhoods so go ahead and begin pulling together marketing material. The Chamber of Commerce might be able to provide some useful resources.

Get Licensed.

Every state has it is own set of requirements to be a licensed real estate professional. Please read the map I've put together and click in your state to visit your state educational requirements. Math is often a sticking point for some agents during the exam so I've written several Real Estate Math posts to greatly help aspiring real estate professionals.

Starting a real Estate Business

Starting a real estate business requires lots of work, training and time. Although the laws vary in each state, starting an actual estate business is normally a three-step process that can take at the very least couple of years. Before beginning your personal company, you need to become a licensed real estate broker, and before becoming a broker, you truly must be a licensed sales agent.

Planning

Whether you're starting a genuine estate business, a large part coffee shop, or an organization that manufactures rocket parts, it's smart to write a business plan. Business planning makes you more successful it is been scientifically proven!

Not only can working through the planning process prompt you to definitely think of essential things like how you're positioned to contend with similar businesses, and exactly how much cash you'll want to actually get started, it will also allow you to validate your idea and get into a habit of setting goals and milestones.

Based on real estate investor Eric Bowlin, the purpose of a business plan is twofold. He says, "First, it provides you a method to formalize your targets and direction. More to the point, it really is a document that you could provide to lenders or investors to clearly illustrate not just your direction but what your location is and how you've got there." During the planning process, Eric got a lot of great advice from an area small company Development Center.

When you haven't had any experience in the actual estate industry, it's smart to get advice from anyone who has. Real estate agent Jamal Asskoumi of Castle Smart says, "If you yourself are in a roundabout way involved in real estate, then it's better to find someone who is, in the planning stage. They'll know far more of the do's and dont's."

Of course, you might always go down the route of taking formal courses on the topic, or reading the best books.

Market research and idea validation

How do you know you've got a thought that will work? How will you know you've picked a distinct segment into the real estate market that truly has a target audience? How will you work out how to position yourself through this niche?

These questions and many more like them could be answered within the initial market research phase. By conducting both primary and secondary marketing research, you give yourself a broader idea of set up target audience you've picked is valuable enough to pursue.

Needless to say, there's no one-fits-all method of figuring out what niche you're best served to help and the selection of responses we got from real estate agents across the United States is proof of that.

Do general market trends early

Finding the time to do your market research early may also help you save both time and money. Michelle Stansbury, an agent at Bluegrass Partners Trust Realty says, "My first year was lots of fumbling around figuring out what didn't work. My second year I tripled my business."

Do market research to assess your personal skills

Brad Pauly, who owns Pauly Presley Realty, took exactly the same learning from your errors approach however for him, it had been a great way to figure out his own strengths and weaknesses. "I figured out my target audience through trial and error," he says. "When I started in the industry, I wouldn't turn away any business! Once I realized my strong suits, I centered on them. Four years when I was licensed, I obtained my broker's license and created the company we have today."

If you're not clear on your own personal strengths and weaknesses, conducting a SWOT analysis will allow you to figure them out.

Get some good real-world experience or find a mentor

If you're a doer first, another approach to market research is to simply get in there and start doing things. A lot of people don't have the excess time or money to work on this, however if you do, good for you, it's as valid a way as any. Morgan Franklin, an authorized real estate agent based out of Lexington, Kentucky, says, "I became confident [my idea] would definitely work because I had already developed enough business to pay most of my startup expenses before I took my real estate exam."

However, Morgan did spend some time employed by a real estate attorney so he previously a bit of know-how before diving in. "If you've got no experience, I would strongly urge a fresh agent to find a mentor to work with for the first couple of years," he suggests. If you haven't had much exposure to the industry, going the "mentor" route is a great idea.

Having said that, Morgan did do a fair bit of research himself. When asked how he figured out who his target audience was, he responded, "I looked over the volume of sales in my city, from the property valuation administrator, after which looked for the 'sweet spot.' That is where the majority of the amount of transactions was occurring. After that, I aimed when it comes to top end of the group."

Cheryl Julcher, the Managing Broker at Yellow Brick Properties, did her general market trends, but also decided to begin in an area she felt passionate about. "Here at Yellow Brick, many of us are about healthy, safe, comfortable, and smart homes eco-conscious and sustainable housing," she explains.

"We went with this passion, which is what I would advise you to do," says Cheryl. "Go with all the market sector millennials, empty nesters, etc. that you care about the essential and therefore are most experienced in."

When you have strong feelings about a specific sector, odds are it is a great spot to at the very least start doing all of your researching the market.

Branding

Branding is important for businesses of each size. If you've got a memorable brand, it is better to build credibility, look bigger than you are, attract customers, as well as in general end up being the first person or company people think about.

According to branding expert Sara Conte of Brand Genie, "Although it is possible to influence your brand through well-designed logos, hilarious ad campaigns, carefully crafted pr announcements, or super-friendly service, ultimately, your brand is exactly what the surface world says it really is."

Essentially, your reputation is the brand.

Branding tip 1: Your reputation is perhaps all down seriously to your relationships

Real estate agent Jamal Asskoumi, of Castle Smart, knows this well; not merely does he have confidence in the necessity of setting yourself apart from the competition, but also into the need for your relationships together with your clients.

"When branding in real estate, make an effort to allow it to be as personal as you can. That is a company which relies heavily on interaction and building relationships. Ensure your business exudes the same welcoming smile you have."

Be someone people would you like to align themselves with. You may be the brand, all things considered.

Realtor Tim Frie takes this idea a step further. He says, "Building a reputation is much more important than building a brand in real estate...plus, building a reputation is easier than constructing a brandname."

Branding tip 2: Provide value and present people what they need

Reputation and authenticity appear to go in conjunction in real estate. Michael Kelczewski a realtor for Brandywine Fine Properties Sotheby's International, feels that folks can sense non-verbal cues and behavior patterns. As a result, there's much less that may go wrong if you behave authentically.

Real estate investor, Eric Bowlin, holds the exact same belief. "Real estate is actually about people a lot more than the land," he says. "As a small company in real estate, i believe it is more info on branding yourself than branding the company. Make people want to work well with you."

Branding tip 3: Creatively create your own space

If, however, you take pride in having the creative chops to brand a thing that sticks out since it's new and innovative, you have a unique opportunity.

Cheryl Julcher of Yellow Brick Properties differentiated her brand from competitors by developing a brandname of homes called Zoetic Homes™. "Each home comes with a nutrition label, is quality verified by an independent alternative party, and it is going to have a design that matches actual performance."

Branding tip 4: end up being the go-to expert

Being a specialist in your industry is yet another great way to set yourself apart. For Morgan Franklin, the secret ingredients were video and an energetic social media marketing presence.

"I have branded myself as a local expert and now have differentiated myself through the use of social networking, and more specifically, video," says Morgan. "I host a weekly real estate show this is certainly published to YouTube and Facebook. It has been huge since it has associated my brand with higher-end properties and even though We haven't had those listings."

Regarding the flipside, if you're young and inexperienced, you have of the same quality an opportunity to sell yourself. "Sell your inexperience (and youth if it applies to you) as a secured item," says agent Michelle Stansbury. "You would be hungry to succeed and are usually more likely to work harder to have homes sold as compared to agents who have already 'made it.' Inexperience isn't a total weakness and don't let anyone convince you it is."

Making it legal

One of the best aspects of engaging in real estate is the fact that for many states, there's really only 1 exam you'll want to pass. Study hard, and also you might possibly take action in a couple of months. Naturally, this differs slightly from state to mention, so be sure to check in with your state about regulations and rules.

In Florida, for example, you don't need to be an agent or a brokerage in order to open up a proper estate company. Based on Tim Frie, "You just need a broker-of-record that is an officer or manager regarding the company that is in charge of overseeing those things and transactions associated with the sales associates."

Of course, real estate qualifications aside, there are several things that you can do pretty early on, including finding out a name for the business, registering said name, applying for a Federal Tax ID, and obtaining any necessary business licenses and permits.

Choosing a business name is a strategic action. Plenty of notable real estate companies are named similar to this: Coldwell Banker, Keller William, Engel & Volkers, Long, and Foster. Not only did you want to emulate what was already proven on the market, but through the way that we offer service, we wanted something very deep to leave behind as a legacy which was due to our time and effort and dedication."

A great many other real estate agents also simply opt for their particular name, because it's a great way to attach your online business to your private brand.

Providing you know very well what things you ought to get done to start, the entire process of actually starting out is not all that hard. "Create a corporation, register your DBA, be sure you are in good standing with all boards and commissions," says Brad Pauly owner of Pauly Presley Realty, listing some key things you need to do to begin with. He also advises aspiring entrepreneurs to appear into getting liability insurance. That's key!

If you're still worried about how to start and how to really make it "legal," real estate broker James Brooks advises consulting a legal professional who focuses primarily on real estate law.

Getting financed

One of many great things about getting started in the real estate industry is that having plenty of cash on hand isn't always necessary.

It's also a company you could start part-time while you're still holding down a day job (though of course, you may need a flexible employer so you duck aside to occasionally take phone calls).

Joshua Jarvis, the master of Jarvis Team Realty, says, "The startup cost to launch in real estate is extremely low. I used the savings I experienced as well as for lower than $1,000 I happened to be in a position to start. Now my monthly budget is 10 times this, you don't actually need any money to start—or so most think."

The real thing to give some thought to, according to Joshua, is cash flow. "Don't just calculate the startup cost, calculate 'carrying cost,'" he says. "As in, exactly how many months it takes you to definitely start cash flowing. In real estate, you will find an excellent 60 days or even more before you might get paid."

For Hollywood real estate professional, Gwen Banta, having the finances to use the job seriously had a great deal to do with other revenue streams in the first place, including her act as an actress and writer.

When you do realize that you want investor funding or a bank loan, writing a company plan is a good first step.

Real estate professional Jamal Asskoumi, took the finances for his business from personal savings. "If you can't fund the project yourself, ensure you discover how and how to locate investors," he says. "Also, create a flawless business plan to present in their mind."

If you're wondering what a proper estate business strategy looks like, take a good look at a few of our free trial realtor industry plans. They'll offer you a good idea of simple tips to structure your personal plan.

Setting up shop

For many people getting started in real estate, an office location is not necessary. As of this beginning phase, the focus is actually more about building a reputation in your chosen niche.

Real estate investor Eric Bowlin says, "The vast majority of people I know who work with real estate have started in their own home. It's more important to choose a target market rather than bother about a place for your storefront. At startup, you have to be flexible and in a position to rapidly adjust your plan if it's no longer working. A physical location will tie you down seriously to that market and make you less flexible while simultaneously adding expenses."

Of course, there may come an occasion once you do would you like to find a business location, hire employees, and get set up because of the right technology. Then again, hiring employees isn't for all. Eric says, "I've had employees in the past and I will not hire an employee again. The government regulations for employees is way too burdensome and expensive. Instead, everyone I work with is treated like a contractor and given a 1099."

In terms of technology, great customer relationship management software and a shared inbox solution is apparently the true estate agent's prized possession. Cheryl Julcher doesn't mince her words: "Our essential technology is our CRM, while the capability to work from anywhere 24/7."

And she's not the only one who advises using an instrument that helps you manage your contacts. For owner Joshua Jarvis, a beneficial CRM is practically indispensable, and it's something many real estate agents overlook. "The only real little bit of technology that might not be wise practice is a database. Whether it's an advanced CRM or simply Outlook, this can be huge. Your database is the business."

If you haven't been already convinced, doing well in real estate boils down to those personal connections you create, whether or perhaps not you've got a real-life office location. When you do hire employees, make certain they're a good fit along with your values as well as your brand first. All things considered, you don't wish to damage the truly amazing reputation you've spent a great deal time building.

Marketing and launching

Ask any real estate professional how they market their business, and you'll realize that "SEO" and "a good web presence" are common responses. Beyond the necessary networking you'll need to do, maintaining an online business in your real estate niche is key to your success.

Again, we get back to the importance of your own personal relationships with people. Getting business is all about seeing people, wherever these are typically, though it is equally important to possess an online presence to make certain that people can find you themselves!

Tim Frie says, "A large amount of real estate marketing is dependent on forming relationships, and you can do this most efficiently by blending an on-line strategy with a normal outreach and connection strategy."

If you don't have any customers, a great place to begin would be to reach out to people in your existing network. "Tell them in what you're doing," Tim says. "Ask when they know anyone who you are able to provide value to. If you're new and starting out, you need to put yourself in situations that enable you to definitely create new connections, meet new people, and supply value just by being yourself. Once people like you, they'll correlate your name with 'real estate' when they themselves or someone they know want to purchase or sell a house."

Career in Real Estate

A lifetime career in real estate can be both rewarding and challenging. Many people earn six-figure salaries, others, just a couple of thousand each year. Although it may be a good career: challenging, flexible and exciting, it's not for all. Here's what you need to know before you receive started in real estate.

Employed by Yourself

As a realtor, you're essentially doing work for yourself. Though there might be a few jobs available that pay an hourly rate, a normal real estate agent works strictly on commissions generated through the sale or rental of a residential or commercial property. In the same way you would before starting any business, you should make sure you've got the right character traits to operate on your own before becoming a real estate agent. You need to be:

- Ambitious
- Organized
- Dedicated
- Persevering

- Friendly
- Goal-oriented

A lifetime career in real estate ensures that you'll set your own personal schedule, but you'll need certainly to be organized and ambitious adequate to actually work at your organization every single day. Organization skills are important because you'll be dealing with contract deadlines, client appointments and follow-ups along with other professionals on the go. I asked Rhonda Taylor, a Realtor with Blakemore Real Estate, in Salt Lake City, Utah, for a few advice about starting out in the commercial. She told me:

Rhonda Taylor, Realtor"It's so great because you are your very own boss. You're able to dictate everything about your work day: You get to wake up when you wish, work when you need, work with who you need. The down side to this to that is you have to be really diligent and hold yourself accountable as it can be an easy task to not work when you don't have a boss looking over your shoulder. It's basically owning your own business. You're not planning to make money in the event that you don't work."

Most real estate agents don't make huge commissions throughout their first year. It requires time to build a client base and get familiar with how the business works. If you are going in thinking that it is something you'll try out for a few months, then throw in the towel if you aren't earning some huge cash, real estate may possibly not be for your needs. Before you will get started as an agent, you should ideally have six months to 1 year's worth of living expenses in the bank, which supplies a cushion whilst you build your business.

You'll need certainly to like working closely with people, because real estate sales is focused on helping people buy or sell their homes, so you'll be in frequent experience of clients every day. When asked about working with people, Rhonda said:

"You should be comfortable dealing with people. You have to have a client service mindset and start to become willing to help them when they need you. Whether you're helping a young couple find their first home, or representing a family who is selling their home and relocating, you should be confident, knowledgeable and most importantly, absolutely willing to go the additional mile for individuals."

Finding a brokerage

As a unique agent, you'll work under a genuine estate broker. Brokers have typically been in the business for many years and also have additional training, knowledge and an independent license. They are needed to carry insurance that protects buying and selling clients, in addition to real estate professionals. Brokers oversee agents and review purchase contracts for errors. In the event that you make an error during a transaction plus the case goes to court, your broker's insurance covers legal fees and settlement costs. In short, the broker is ultimately the responsible party in a transaction. In substitution for carrying this responsibility, your broker will require a portion of one's sales commissions and may charge you other fees.

Choosing the best broker is essential for career success. The best broker for you might vary, depending on your previous knowledge, dependence on mentoring and financial expectations. Some brokers are extremely hands-on and provide formal training during your first 12 months in the commercial. Others simply provide insurance and a recognizable brand, but don't expect to spend much time to you.

It's a smart idea to visit several brokers before you get started in your real estate career. By taking a look at what each is offering, you could make the right decision for you personally.

The "Split"

The broker carries the duty for each and every transaction, and spends money on insurance. He also provides a workplace, branding and often marketing. Large national brokerages, such as for example Coldwell Banker or Century 21, advertise on tv, radio plus in print ads. Each local brokerage must pay franchise fees to pay for that marketing. Smaller, local brokerages may not advertise nationally, nevertheless they work tirelessly to create a recognizable brand and often advertise in local publications, on local billboards and by participating in local events. The broker must cover his costs, so he takes a portion of every commission that a realtor earns. This can be called a "split."

When you initially start out in the industry, your portion of the split will undoubtedly be low. You might start off with a 70/30 split, or even as little as 60/40 (you obtain the larger for the two amounts). Needless to say, your broker will be so much more hands-on in the beginning, providing additional training, mentoring and advice.

As you become more experienced and successful, your split goes up. Most brokers have a method put up where, as you reach a certain dollar quantity of sales, you are going into the next level.

Standard splits for successful agents are around 80/20 and certainly will be up to 90/10.

How Much Cash Can You Make?

Most real estate professionals are paid completely on commission. In residential real estate transactions, your home seller typically pays around 6% for the sales price towards the agent(s) who handle the sale (Commission rates vary slightly, but 6% is common). The two agents split the commission, then that amount is split because of the broker. Here's an example:

Joe lists Sally's house for $100,000. Mike brings his clients to see the home and his clients end up buying it. Following the transaction closes, Joe receives $3,000 and thus does Mike. Both Joe and Mike work on an 80/20 split with regards to brokers. So, each receive a commission look for $2400. They'll be responsible for paying income taxes on that amount.

How much money you'll make is based on two factors:

1) The housing marketplace, including the availability of virginia homes and the availability of mortgage loans for prospective buyers.

2) Your ambition. The more you work, the more money you'll make.

"There are countless possibilities. Your earnings isn't limited. It depends as to how hard you intend to work and what you want to put into it. Just how many jobs exist where you are able to earn a six-figure income without a college degree? That doesn't mean that you don't need an education, though. You'll have to set up lots of time learning about the business, about the real estate market and about techniques like marketing and networking. It's an education… just not on a college campus!"

What you ought to Get Going

Getting into a real estate career is relatively inexpensive, when compared with other businesses. Here's what you'll have to start:

Real Estate License:

Though requirements vary from state-to-state, all require licensing. Consult your local Board of Realtors or your state's Department of Real Estate to learn what you need to do to obtain a license. Typically, you'll be expected to go to training classes. Then you'll take a situation exam. Once you've passed, you'll pay a fee and receive a license. Most states require also continuing education and license renewal.

MLS Access:

The MLS (Multiple Listing Service), is a comprehensive online tool that allows agents to find properties for purchasing clients, and list properties for selling clients. The MLS charges a monthly fee for access.

Board of Realtor Dues:

if you opt to join the Board of Realtors, you'll pay annual dues. Though it is not mandatory that you join, most real estate professionals do. Look at the National Association of Realtors site for more information on the benefits of becoming a Realtor®.

Computer:

Ideally, a laptop that you could take to you towards the office also to client meetings.

Smart Phone:

You'll be from the phone a lot as a realtor, taking calls from clients, getting updates from appraisers, home inspectors and loan officers, and setting appointments with potential new clients. Get a model with GPS so that you can easily find addresses when taking buyer clients to look at homes. You'll also be able to remain in contact via email and text, and that can look up properties when you look at the MLS (Multiple Listing Service).

Car:

While you don't need a fancy car, it should be in reasonable working condition. Ensure that is stays neat and clutter-free; you'll drive clients around occasionally.

Business Cards:

While many people don't make use of these any more, they're still a staple for real estate agents.

Signage:

You'll need signs to market homes for sale, open houses and other events. Design your own signs utilizing your broker's logo (generally in most states this really is required). Consult your state's Real Estate Division for any other items to include on your own sign that may be required by law.

Spend money on a variety of signage: directional signs to help people find your listings, vinyl banners for larger-format advertising and car magnets to alert people that you are a realtor. Some signs can be made to work with every property (such as for instance directional signage). Others must certanly be designed especially for one listing (list the features, price and address of a home, by way of example).

Clothing:

Dressing professionally is essential when you look at the realtor industry. Spend money on some nice suits, quality shoes and accessories in order for you'll look nice and feel confident.

Get Going!

If you were to think that a vocation in real estate is a good fit for you personally, get going! Are you when you look at the real estate industry?

Real Estate Commission Rates

Real estate commissions are one of the more debated factors in selling a house. So, should home sellers be paying commissions after all? What's really reasonable? How can homeowners get the best mixture of value and net proceeds?

- Real Estate Commissions Because Of The Numbers
- 89% of home sellers are employing real estate professionals
- The typical rate of commission is 6% of this closing price
- Luxury real estate specialists often charge 10%
- The standard commission on rentals is 10% for the lease

Where Does the Money Go?

Some genuinely believe that Realtor rates are costly. The information shows that the typical agent barely makes minimum wage. So, where does the cash go?

Buyer & Seller Agent Splits

The gross commission is typically split 50/50 between the agents who represent the buyer and seller. So, out of a gross 6% commission, your agent would only typically get 3% gross.

Brokerage Splits

Out of that 3% the agent needs to split with their office. This generally ranges from a 50/50 to as high as a 90/10 split. So, on average the actual agent may only get 1.5% of that 6% commission.

Agent Costs

Then the agent has to cover their costs. That means office fees, technology fees, license fees, marketing, and insurance fees. Then there are the specific costs they need to spend money on for your house. They've been betting this cash on their capability to market your house, and they're doing it out of their own pocket upfront. Between transportation, signs, open houses, printing flyers, newspaper and magazine ads, photography, and internet marketing, this will probably easily be thousands of dollars. That is just the tip regarding the iceberg of what great agents will do as well.

On a $100,000 home sale, at a 6% gross commission rate, the agent may only get $1,500 BEFORE a few of these costs come out. That doesn't include income taxes either. Most might turn out to be out of pocket on a transaction such as this. Which may be different on a $1M home, however the expenses do rise because of the level of a home being marketed on the market too. Consider that a single page ad on a top-level website or newspaper can very quickly run $5,000 to $7,000 alone.

Being fair; in fact most agents are probably vastly underpaid. That's one of many reasons that 90% of the latest agents go broke within their first year.

In the event that you just make an effort to sell yourself; which means investing in every associated with the marketing yourself, and spending money on it upfront. Plus, you'll definitely need an actual estate attorney to greatly help negotiate, complete contracts, and accompany you at the closing. Once you start marketing you'll also realize that you might be mostly approached by Realtors, plus they aren't going to show your property with their interested and qualified buyers unless you agree to pay a commission.

Then you will find FSBO websites or flat fee MLS services that may list your home on their sites, or sell you DIY marketing materials. Again, this really is an upfront investment, with no guarantee of results. Whatever they don't typically tell you is that no one will probably show your premises, until you offer commission to buyers' agents. Like it or not, many agents will curate the menu of homes they show their customers on the basis of the commission offered. So, to make this work, expect to offer 3%. The downside is you continue to have no representation, or qualified advice, but your buyer does. For in-depth breakdown of additional reasons as to why, visit our article 11 main reasons why FSBO Sellers Should Reconsider Hiring an agent.

Note, that the master of one of the largest FSBO services ironically used an agent for the sale of his very own home.

It's Exactly About the Web

All sorts of things that it's exactly about the net. A part of this is basically the net proceeds. If just how much you are going to place in your pocket on closing day is exactly what is most significant, it doesn't matter if an agent charges 1% or 10%. It is about this net number. Some agents just have more established networks and so are better sales people. They could negotiate higher sales prices.

Then there is also the internet value. Your net proceeds are a part of this. So, is how quickly you sell, and just how the ability is. Every day you wait to market costs money. If an individual agent charges a little more but sells your house 2 months faster, they may be the most effective deal. Then sellers should take into account how professional the agent is supposed to be, and how seamless they can make the process.

Commission Rates Are Negotiable

Everything is negotiable in real estate therefore we have tactics to how to go about achieving this within our article just how to Negotiate Commission Rates with Real Estate Agents. Don't discount using an agent as you think you must pay 6% to 10% in commissions. Agents may negotiate lower rates with regards to the variety of transaction, the services required, and frequency of business.

For example; if you should be an actual estate investor buying and selling 10 homes four weeks, a real estate agent may be willing to work a 50% off deal in return for the quantity. If they're receiving a referral from a reliable source they could offer a modest discount, while still giving a full-service experience. If you don't require the agent to host open houses, and so they can secure a buyer directly, without the need to split with another agent, chances are they may offer a price reduction relative to their savings.

Bonuses & Incentives

Home sellers might also work with their agents on bonuses and incentives. These could be paid by the seller, or out from the listing agent's commission. As an example; offering a $10,000 bonus for a complete price offer which closes within 1 month, or contributing 3% of the purchase price toward buyer's closing costs.

Real estate commission rates

In accordance with the National Association of Realtors 87% of home buyers come through an agent. Between this fact, while the net numbers and value provided by good agents, even standard commission rates could possibly be cheap. Still, there clearly was room to negotiate, and thousands of dollars may be saved by getting top agents to compete through the UpNest.com platform.

Is career as a Real Estate Agent Right for you

A lot of people think that a real estate career is simple money, and it will be usually before long. And there's much more to it than that.

You don't need to be a "salesperson" which will make a good residing in this field. Real estate is primarily a site business, so serving your customers well contributes to your success. But the majority of people have found real estate to be an all natural transition from another sales career plus they believe that it really is more fulfilling. After all, you are helping people with what exactly is often one of several largest financial transactions they're going to make inside their lives.

Needless to say, every career has drawbacks. It is a matter of balancing the great from the bad and gauging your tolerance for the bad. You are your own boss as a real estate agent, but this comes with a great deal of added responsibility and a little bit of a cash investment to begin with.

Education Requirements Can Be Minimal

Its not necessary a college degree to be a real estate agent, although education is normally helpful in any career you pursue. States almost universally require which you have at the least a higher school diploma or GED, and you needs to be at least 18 yrs old. Some states have training requirements and you will need certainly to pass a licensing exam, but you can repeat this in significantly less time than it will require to make a bachelor's degree.

Starting out, you'll almost certainly need certainly to complete a pre-licensing course, nevertheless the investment of time could be minimal, as little as 30 days from start to finish. The exam itself can be challenging in a few states. It's often divided in to a state-level section with a second part aimed at national laws and issues, and you will need certainly to pass both.

The National Association of Realtors regularly sponsors courses as you are able to enroll in to prepare yourself, and they're going to look great on the resume, too.

The Cash Is Great, Eventually

You're typically stuck with similar wage or salary week in and week out once you work the standard job, unless and until your employer chooses to be magnanimous and offer you a raise. Any limits to your eventual earnings are the ones you add in position yourself if you are a real estate agent. Exactly how much you get is commonly directly proportional to exactly how much and just how hard you work.

Having said that, the word "eventual" is key here. You won't reap a windfall very first week face to face. It simply does not happen by doing this, and you should be ready to deal with that. It can come down seriously to your temperament and your tolerance for just a little financial stress.

You'll have to spend some money to get started. There is the licensing exam and any training you will need to start. You will also need business cards, an advertising budget, and a good, reliable car. And you will have all your very own bills to cover as well.

Some experts' advise that it could 6 months to a year before you receive very first commission check because commissions are usually paid at the conclusion of transactions. You will need to put in a fair little bit of work to arrive at that time, and you will need ample savings to survive through that time.

Real estate professionals earn a median salary of approximately $47,880 at the time of 2017, in line with the Bureau of Labor Statistics. Median implies that 1 / 2 of all agents make a lot more than this and half earn less. And also this encompasses people who regularly deal in seven-figure properties along with agents who dabble in the field part-time. The two extremes tend to balance out the numbers.

You'll Enjoy Flexible Hours, Sometimes

This perk comes with a caveat, too, also it comes down to what's vital that you you. Nobody will probably require that you punch an occasion clock at 9 a.m. and stay planted at your desk until 5 p.m., Monday through Friday. You are able to set your personal hours, and you can move them around to support your personal needs. If you like to grab your youngster from school, you are able to do that.

The flip side is the fact that nearly all your real estate clients is supposed to be punching time clocks or will likely to be otherwise confined to create working schedules. You will need to make your self available if they are if you wish to do a great business. This often means working nights, weekends, as well as some holidays.

You're Helping People

The helping facet of real estate work is a big advantage for altruistic types. Your clients are on the verge of taking what might be the most important financial step up their lives, perhaps buying their first home or selling their long-time family home to downsize since they're retiring. In any case, you may expect nerves and often buyers' or sellers' remorse.

You do not need a Ph.D. in psychology to manage all of this, but having plenty of compassion and patience can really help, especially if you prefer giving freely of both.

The Tech Advantage

Technology advances and also the mobile world will help agents that aren't exceptionally people-oriented to be successful in real estate. When you can work a great website that's mobile device-friendly, if you can handle some social website posting, and in case you respond quickly to emails or text messages, you should have a genuine opportunity to relate genuinely to prospects.

The professionals of a Real Estate Career

You'll probably find very diverse cause of choosing an actual estate career if you question a team of brand-new agents. Many love the helping nature of this job, although some desire to exercise their independent nature and start to become their own bosses. But it takes commitment and a good investment of effort, time, and money to create an effective real estate career.

You'll get a whole lot in return. You are an unbiased contractor, so you can control your own business. Your earnings isn't limited. It is predicated on your talent and your work ethic. It is possible to build future business with great service and client referrals.

The Cons of a vocation in Real Estate

If you're an unbiased contractor, you're on your own with regards to making certain your business thrives. Income could be quite a while in coming when you first start off. The first months and years in real estate could be feast or famine before you get going.

There is a top failure rate for new agents. Liability and risk are part of representing clients. You'll need insurance because some mistakes, such as for example neglecting to disclose a material fact about the property or neglecting inspections, will get you sued.

Pros:

- You're an Independent Contractor and control your own business.
- Your income is not limited & based on your skills and work ethic.
- Set your personal working arrangements and vacations.
- Work outdoors as well as in varied locations.
- Build future business with great service and client referrals.
- Enjoy helping people in another of their largest financial transactions.

Cons:

- You're an Independent Contractor as well as on your own to understand the business.

- Income can be a long time getting going and "feast or famine".
- You need to be available if the clients would like you.
- There's a top failure rate for new agents.
- Liability and risk are part of representing clients.

Real Estate Careers For those who don't want to buy and sell Homes

Whenever you think of a proper estate professional, you likely get an extremely specific image of a residential real estate professional, helping people purchase and sell their homes and performing all of the related tasks. This is certainly definitely the best-known real estate career, however it's not the only person.

If you can find components of a residential real estate sales career that are appealing to you and others which are not, perchance you will be better designed for an alternative career path in real estate. Lets explore some of the lesser-known real estate careers available and help you discover one that is the best fit for your needs.

Commercial Real Estate Salesperson

Commercial real estate professionals help clients lease, buy, and sell commercial property. There are lots of similarities between commercial and residential agents, but there are several unique differences as well. For one, the commercial real estate sales process often takes more than the residential process. And also the needs and concerns associated with clients you certainly will serve are not the same.

Both residential and commercial real estate careers require that you earn your real estate salesperson's license. Legally, there isn't any post-secondary education necessary to become a commercial real estate agent in most states. However, most commercial brokerages expect their candidates to at the least have a bachelor's degree. Like a residential agent, commercial agents must "hang their license" with (work beneath) an agent. You can find out about the commercial real estate career path in this essay.

Real Estate Broker

An actual estate broker owns and runs a proper estate brokerage company. To become a broker, you must earn an enhanced license. Every state's rules are very different, but must require that you log a prescribed length of time as an authorized agent before you can earn a broker's license. Real estate brokers operate independently, which means that they keep 100% of these commission split. They often times likewise have real estate professionals working under them inside their office, who they hire, support, and manage. There was a substantial number of responsibility that comes with running a brokerage. As a result, some brokers choose not to represent clients within the sale or purchase of real estate and dedicate most of their energy to running an effective brokerage.

Business Broker

Business brokers aid and assist buyers and sellers within the purchase of businesses. At first, this may seem like the exact same job as a commercial real estate professional, however it's not. For example, commercial agents could be in charge of selling a dental office. But a company broker would sell the business that occupies that office along with the property. Some states require a license to become a small business broker. Even if you live in a state that will not require one, it is recommended that real estate professionals complete specialized business broker training to achieve success at it.

Loan Officer

Loan officers play a critical role in the real estate transaction process, since most buyers will demand that loan which will make a proper estate purchase. There are loan officers who focus on both mortgage (residential) and commercial lending. They work for lending institutions, like banks, and work as an intermediary amongst the consumer plus the lending institution. They work to comprehend their clients' needs and supply lending solutions tailored to your individual or company they're serving. When an ideal option is identified, in addition they assist individuals in the application for the loan process.

Home Inspector

It is incredibly rare today for a house to sell without a home inspection. Home inspectors examine, analyze, and report regarding the physical condition of a residential property. They play a crucial role in presenting most of the details about the home, therefore the buyers can make a decision about whether or not to go forward making use of their planned purchase. Home inspection professionals often (not always) begin their career in another of the building trades. When they actually choose to be a house inspector, they typically complete education to learn more about home systems these are generally not really acquainted with therefore the particulars of running a house inspection business. Some states require home inspectors to complete education and be licensed, while other states try not to.

Real Estate Appraiser

Real estate appraisers provide an estimate of land and building value before real estate is sold, developed, mortgaged, taxed, or insured. Because there are so many factors that influence the value of property, including specific local market conditions, real estate appraisers typically practice in an exceedingly specific and defined geographic location. Real estate appraisers are required to complete specific education and meet licensure requirements to practice within their profession.

Real Estate Assistant

Real estate assistants make use of agents and brokers to serve clients and manage the day-to-day tasks associated with helping them buy and sell real estate. The amount of service an assistant can offer without a license varies from state to state. That is why, some agents and brokers prefer to hire assistants that have earned their license. Real estate practitioners vary in how they pay their real estate assistants. Some pay a predictable hourly wage or salary. Others offer a commission split.

Real Estate Developer

Real estate development is a career field that requires the vision to consider a blank canvas of land and imagine what it could be. Many tasks fall under the umbrella of real estate development, & most developers do a little mixture of them. Developers purchase land, finance deals, and manage the growth plan for a given bit of real estate from just starting to end. Real estate development is normally a high-risk, high-reward career. Developers shoulder all the front-end investment, but ultimately maximize the worthiness associated with the land prior to taking that space to advertise. If they've done their homework and demand can there be when it comes to specific property they've developed, there's an important financial opportunity waiting for them in the back end.

House Flipper

Reality television has made the phrase "flipping a house" something all of us understand. If you're just the right person for this type of work, it may be quite lucrative. However, as we've also learned from reality television, the number of individuals who are actually good at flipping houses is significantly smaller than how many individuals who think they're good at it. House flippers typically purchase a house centered on potential. They invest in improving the property through their particular (or hired) labor and ultimately try to resell the home for a profit.

Landlord or Property Manager

Landlords own property they rent to tenants. That property can consist of land, commercial buildings, apartments, and houses. Property managers work on behalf of a landlord to perform many different services that will include marketing rentals, maintenance and upkeep, rent collection, giving an answer to tenant concerns, and also handling evictions. While many landlords hire property managers or property management companies, additionally, it is not unusual for a landlord to behave because their own property manager.

How to Finance Your Real Estate Business

Hard Money Lender

Hard money lenders are a financing tactic often employed by real estate investors. Instead of coming from a bank, the funds for those investments originate from a personal individual or group. Because these loans do not need to go through any corporate procedures, they frequently have looser qualifying requirements and may be secured faster. Additionally, private lenders may be much more available to backing risky projects.

Knowing that, investors should always be confident within their ability to pay back the loan quickly before signing regarding the dotted line. Hard money loans often have very high rates of interest and require a big down payment or personal collateral. They likewise have much shorter terms than traditional loans, averaging only per year or two.

Microloans

Microloans are generally geared toward newer businesses or startups that need capital to come up with further growth. Whilst the name suggests, these loans are smaller than what's usually offered with traditional bank financing. Lower balances mean that microloan programs are less limiting in terms of their qualifying requirements like credit rating, which is often a comfort to those concerned with borrowing above their means.

However, microloans may possibly not be a great fit for all. Though these loans can go up to $50,000, the common loan is only about $13,000, therefore it's crucial that you gauge overhead costs accordingly. Also, their attention rates are typically greater than those offered through standard loan programs.

Real Estate Crowdfunding

In the past, investing in real estate was restricted to individuals with deep pockets, but because the passage of the 2012 JOBS Act, crowdfunding has grown to become an easy method for investors to diversify their portfolios at a far lower cost. In place of being forced to search out and restore properties by themselves, investors can browse crowdfunding platforms to select from a listing of available investment projects for which to participate. They then are able to finance shares of the property at the lowest cost sometimes as little as $1,000 and collect a percentage regarding the profits or rent payments when the project has been completed.

Having said that, this kind of investing does come with elevated risk. Investors have significantly less control of the outcome than they might in a traditional fix-and-flip scenario. Be aware that there could be a longer wait for profits on return, depending on how each deal is structured. Additionally, understand that if the project fails, it is the investors that will shoulder the loss as opposed to the builder. You are able to find out more about crowdfunding in this in-depth article.

SBA Loans

SBA loans are so-named as the Small Business Association offers a warranty of repayment to banks which can be willing to underwrite loans for new entrepreneurs. The guarantee lets banks become more willing to take risks. As the affordability of a loan depends on an investor's unique situation, generally these loans have higher borrowing limits up to $2,000,000. SBA loans also come with longer terms, lower down payments, and protection against balloon payments, which will help businesses maintain a reliable cash flow.

It's important to see SBA loans can't be used to spend money on real estate but can be employed to start an actual estate business, such as a brokerage or property management fund. Unfortunately, the security that SBA loans offer comes at a cost. Not only is it at the mercy of high fees, investors should have a top credit score and also show significant profit to their tax returns in order to qualify. The applying process can also be lengthy and requires the borrower to put on personal assets as collateral.

ROBS

If applying for that loan just isn't for you personally, a rollover as business startup (ROBS) provider may be the best choice. This method of financing allows small business owners to attract funds from existing retirement accounts without incurring tax or withdrawal penalties. Considering that the cash is their particular, there aren't any debt payments, leaving them absolve to invest the total amount into business growth. Also, in the event that the business enterprise should fail, this leaves no negative effect on their credit rating or any other assets.

Before committing to a ROBS strategy, an investor needs to be certain to weigh the risks. Regarding the one hand, they may be able only draw the money inside their existing accounts, which means their available funds can be smaller than they might be with a loan. Consistent with that, if the investor chooses to invest the entirety of their retirement funds to the business, therefore the business fails, they may be left without security in retirement. Just like SBA loans, ROBS is not used to purchase real estate.

Real Estate and Artificial Intelligence

"An Artificial Intelligence (AI) may be the science & designing of creating intelligent machines, mainly intelligent PC programs" – in accordance with the father of Artificial Intelligence John McCarthy. This is the solution to making software or a computer robot that will think intelligently like a person. It will be the notion of having machines that may feel like a human.

Nowadays artificial intelligence is changing the world in lot of ways. It is about making our lives better yet than before. There are lots of companies are receiving success considerably by way of artificial intelligence. One of many growing companies is real estate.

Today AI is not taking the host to real estate agents. The technology like AI helps them to truly save time & money as well. We're going to discuss the benefits of real estate and artificial intelligence.

Artificial intelligence will alter the real estate industry:

Nowadays there is absolutely no doubt that artificial intelligence will alter all in the real estate. Let's see how artificial intelligence will alter the true estate industry:

Data Management:

Many realtors manage huge amounts of information. The total of data is increasing from year to year. In the event that human realtors do this entire work by hand – it takes sufficient time to manage it. Into the real estate professionals frequently requires the data in regards to the property. You can automate data collection & data management through artificial intelligence (AI).

Getting Data-Driven Insights:

Artificial intelligence (AI) receives the exact same patterns when you look at the data, although that data is not yet determined. Even experience realtors sometimes are helpless to recognize complex patterns. Another issue isn't just to find the data but in addition to obtain insights as a result. Artificial intelligence person finds the specific area is most likely to explode in popularity in later.

Property Price Calculations:

There's a challenge when you look at the real estate sector: it really is quite difficult to calculate the worth of this property. Generally, the true estate agents find out the cost according to the former sales costs without taking into consideration many points.

These points are including neighborhoods, environment changes, improvements, infrastructure, and transportation and so on. Every one of these features influence the finish property value. Artificial Intelligence can resolve that problem with pattern identification by exposing the points that impact the property cost.

Lead Management:

Lead management was the center of every company & business into the Real Estate is not the particular case. Artificial Intelligence or AI may process plenty of data when you look at the search for vital information. Realtors and other marketing agency use that data in marketing functions like advertising, post-sales, pre-sales an such like. That data assists the real estate agents to obtain the property clients most likely to buy.

Customers Interaction:

Nowadays people face the latest, unsighted before, chatbots that use natural language processing and artificial intelligence. That chatbots work quickly and smartly to process complicated user queries. That chatbots are self-learned. Chatbots can learn into the way of human communication.

Reduces the cost of real estate services:

You are able to save switch office from offline to online offices by making use of artificial intelligence improvement technologies. Thus realtors can reduce their office costs as well as in return provide their services to clients at a low cost.

Helps in the commercial transaction:

Artificial intelligence (AI) can be used in the bank in order to make business deal faster & safer. Also, it can stop cheating by verifying bank accounts & notifying you will find any issues.

How will artificial intelligence in real estate work

Two phrases: Lease Abstraction.

Lease abstraction a method of collecting from a rental agreement for desire to analysis & modeling. Nevertheless, LEVERTON develops the technique with artificial intelligence. Leases are specially made the actual estate sector engaging.

Leases are complicated, and lengthy deeds are generally consisting of a sizable page of data, and examining them may take anywhere from 4 – 8 hours.

Leases could be dropped and pulled into a platform with LEVERTON's artificial intelligence. This may examine those leases and in line with the information you give and that can mechanically pull the data & show them in a talented manner.

These kinds of analytics in real estate save time, lessen the total expense basis, and lastly, give a more well-aimed procedure for lease abstraction.

The true estate sector doesn't have significant technological advancement. Nevertheless the MRI Software brings the way to keep its customers contemporary with great & flexible solutions. Also it helps companies to succeed in the present day time.

LEVERTON is functioning to obtain the new technology to your market by implementing an artificial intelligence that boosts the method of lease abstraction.

Whilst the artificial intelligence of LEVERTON is a time-saving machine, perhaps one of the most valuable & unique attributes of its service is its ability to draw a complete of data from leases & agreements.

This data will give you your company an even more comprehensive snapshot of that rental agreement. It will qualify you to definitely make successful business resolution concerning your property.

The true estate field can just do it utilizing the modern time. And yes it is preparing to meet with the challenges of today using this technological advancement.

What does the industry think?

In accordance with the research among real estate experts on the basis of the current utilization of AI, its future use and what points might stop its acceptance, there are some important aspects about artificial intelligence and realtor industry. These factors will give a clear conception concerning the aftereffect of artificial intelligence throughout the real estate business. They are including:

• There is only one person in five (18%) comment that artificial intelligence will substitute human efficiency in the long run

• More than half (54%) regarding the real estate experts already use artificial intelligence to promote the keyword search system in the realtor industry deal.

• Almost two-thirds of people (69%) trust artificial intelligence provides their company a competitive benefit by qualifying a higher amount and lots of data to be searched at high speed.

• Over fifty-three percent recover too little dependence in artificial intelligence's ability to match human knowledge & decision-making

When asked where AI gets the best influence regarding progressing the competency of processes, over three-quarters of consumer says identifying related data in an important data room. Also, two-thirds of individuals say it really is eliminating time-consuming manual review system.

However, it doesn't mean the battle of technology vs. humans. Irrespective of it is to automate a huge wide range of methods, artificial intelligence (AI) will continue to work best in combination with human efficiency & intelligence.

Artificial intelligence needs to learn from human attitude & there isn't any substitute for years of expertise, knowledge, and inspiration. Nevertheless, artificial intelligence (AI) goes with those aspects and adds massive worth by simply making real estate processes far more efficient, automated and cost-effective.

Real Estate Marketing

Real estate marketing is focused on promoting your brand as a real estate agent and securing buyer and seller leads by sharing your listings on social media, advertising your agency, and building your internet site content. For fresh marketing ideas, take a look at our ultimate range of marketing advice from top-producing agents below.

Market Yourself

The National Association of Realtors (NAR) states that 90% of home buyers house hunt online. While the largest real estate website with more than 160 million visitors per month, Zillow could be the first place you have to be. Zillow Premier Agent is Zillow's platform that lets you advertise on local Zillow and Trulia listings. We estimate that for almost any $1 you may spend, you'll earn $2.60 in commissions. Follow this link to get rates in your town.

Offer Home Valuations to fully capture Seller Leads

The most difficult marketing challenges for real estate agents is capturing seller leads. Real Geeks offers a house valuation tool that you can put right on your site. By inputting a few details, sellers can create a valuation report for his or her property and receive monthly updates. You reap the benefits of collecting these seller email addresses, that are added to your selection of leads. View here for a home valuation tool demo.

Leverage Influencer Marketing

One good way to gain social validity and expand the reach and hype of an inventory is by using influencers and public relations. For example, if a list is unique, you can get in touch with local bloggers and Instagram influencers — whose followership matches your target buyer — and also have them create related content and share it with their followers. There are several websites and blogs which have an apartment of the week showcase that one can try and have your space featured in.

Generate Referrals by Hosting Community Events

My favorite marketing advice would be to embrace community engagement. As an example, in May and June, we host two free community paper shred events — one in Los Alamitos, California, while the other in Brea. The big event reduces paper within the landfill and helps people reduce identity theft. To help spread the phrase, our agents farm various neighborhoods with flyers and door hangers. People can shred up to five boxes of paper at no cost, which will be about a $100 savings.

Make Your Website Your Storefront

Our primary marketing tool is our website. In today's market, it will be the storefront to your company. Having a mobile-friendly site that ranks saturated in organic traffic will surpass all of your paid digital advertising. It not only has to showcase both you and your differentiators, but in addition has to portray attention to detail when promoting your listings. The photography needs to be on point, that you simply will use in every marketing piece, including social networking posts.

Create Real Estate Websites

One of the ways we can generate five or more new leads daily is by using our local community pages. The thing that makes this such a powerful marketing idea may be the fact you might be reverse-engineering focus on generate real estate leads. When you put the work in up front, these leads are continuous.

Provide a Complimentary Moving Truck

My no. 1 marketing idea for real estate is my complimentary moving truck, available for use by clients who buy or sell a home. I also provide the truck for use to nonprofit organizations. It's a moving billboard, and no other agent in the region offers a moving truck. It gets lots of attention.

In addition strategically park it in high-traffic areas when not being used. When events have been in town that focus on homeowners, including the home or boat show, my moving truck will likely to be there.

Use Instagram Stories

Instagram Stories are huge in 2019, given that the sheer number of daily active users of Instagram Stories has surpassed 500 million. The real question is how to use them to offer more homes and grow your local brand recognition. Engagement is absolutely key, so make use of the polls and Q&A stickers within Stories. Ask questions, use GIFs, and make the content as simple to interact with as possible.

The more people you build relationships with, the greater they will remember you, while the more you train the Instagram algorithm that you have great content, which IG will reward with an increase of organic reach than if no one ever engaged with you. You can run contests and giveaways within Instagram Stories. As an example, have people take screenshots of them listening to your podcast, ask them to direct message you the image, and then choose one at random to win something. Master how to get people engaged and coming back for more, and you'll win.

Send Postcards

To offer your postcards staying power, Wachtel recommends using "fridge-worthy" subjects like best metro area hikes, a good go-to recipe for guacamole, helpful tips from what NFL referee signals mean, or advice for timing your Thanksgiving meal perfectly. As she explains, "We regularly hear from clients as well as prospective agents who end up calling us or their agent directly based on a postcard that were hanging to their refrigerator or memo board for months on end."

Optimize Your Facebook Page

With millions of daily users, you'd be remiss not to ever utilize Facebook as a marketing tool these days. Download this free ebook from Matterport to learn about some of the biggest improvements you could make to your company Facebook page, how exactly to set up paid campaigns, and lots of other helpful tips. It also discusses how to convert these contributes to actual sales. Get started today.

Create Subdivision Website Pages

When you may not be able to compete with Zillow for search phrases like "houses on the market in [city]," you might be in a position to rank on Google for more niche search phrases for micro-neighborhoods, pretty streets, or subdivisions. Photos, videos, an industry snapshot, school district information, and pertinent information regarding a subdivision or area are great methods to build organic traffic to your website.

Highlight Homes With Professional Photography

95% of buyers start their search on the internet, plus the quality for the photography should determine if a residential property gets seen or not. It's also a known truth that when the photographs are not excellent, the home buyers won't stop and read the description of the property. Even though a realtor suggests a residential property with their customer, the buyer with a busy schedule will decide based solely on the photos if they like to spend their time planning to visit a property. It's difficult to overcome the first bad reaction even though they do start to see the property.

Use Unique Décor to Set Your Listing Apart

Have one quirky item in the house. Because of this, when buyers are referring to it, they could say, "the house with the giant Buddha" or "the orange rug house." Have a thing that stays inside their mind about the style or design. Sometimes, a perfectly nice, normal house can be forgotten about when it is the middle house of six houses seen through the same day.

Live Stream Your Agency's Day-to-Day

When scrolling through a social media marketing feed, a "Live Now" tag is more or less irresistibly clickable. Folks are naturally curious. Seeing an innovative new listing when it comes to first time? You will want to show your audience via live stream? They'll feel just like they're getting the inside scoop, and you'll be able to grow your audience to get more leads. That's a win-win situation.

In this edition of Beverly Hills superstar broker Peter Lorimer's amazing "Magic Minute" series, he walks you through the process.

Choose Words That Sell

If you're working as a listing agent, it's important to create descriptions which will jump from the page and grab the buyer. A beneficial tactic is always to appeal to the buyer's emotions. Use keywords that paint a photo. It's not only about sharing facts, but additionally about selling stories.

Market Leader enables you to buy actual buyer and seller leads who wish to be contacted by a realtor. This lets you create your stable of leads and target these with compelling listing descriptions. Check to see if Market Leader has leads available in your ZIP code.

Focus Your Marketing Efforts

We have discovered that marketing more often to an inferior geographic area works much better than marketing wide and shallow. We use a mixture of direct mail, calls, targeted search engine optimization (SEO), and pay-per-click (PPC) to find our customers.

Make Connections with Local Businesses

Real estate is a people business. To market yourself successfully also to attract new leads and clients, you first need certainly to make them like you as an individual also to demonstrate to them that you care about the area area and community. Establish relations with the local shopkeepers, business owners, and employees. Take part in local events. A few of these efforts will not only cause you to feel better and more engaged but may also cause you to be noticed off their agents and brokers who aren't so involved in the life of the neighborhood community.

Showcase Your Charitable Side

I believe the simplest way to achieve success at real estate will be supply the prospective customers something to consider you by. Real estate professionals have to differentiate themselves, additionally the solution to accomplish that is through Giveback Homes, which will be an organization of agents that builds homes for people in need. This organization is creating social change, giving real estate professionals a good social platform and ways to differentiate themselves from the competition.

Create a Blog That Answers Client Questions

Real estate is often a hot topic of discussion, so any talking points I'm able to provide in a blog is good reading. We have worked diligently over the past 38 years positioning myself as an industry expert in neuro-scientific luxury residential real estate sales in the Hamptons. Clients and customers desire to hear from me. Whether it is my update on current market conditions or my opinion/personal views on design and architecture. My breadth of business and market knowledge is encapsulated when you look at the data I provide with quotes from me often utilized in the press.

Create a Video Series to generally share With Leads

Social media is a vital option to both remain in touch with individuals you realize and also to ensure you get your name call at front of brand new people. We post regularly on Facebook, Instagram, Twitter, and so on. We do a weekly video series called "Ask the Realtor" we just finished season one and generally are planning season two and turn those short videos into Facebook ads. The videos typically earn around 4,000 views each at about a nickel per view. They've been ideal for exposure to new people within our area.

Stick Out with Handwritten Notes

I would say that my favorite marketing advice is to write thank you notes. I was thinking going the high-tech route when contacting people will be the path to take. I was wrong. People are very receptive to receiving handwritten letters and thank-you notes. It sounds silly and easy, but this old-school technique seems to set me apart from my competition. Very few people are achieving this anymore. In real estate, you need any advantage you could get.

Google Ads

The most effective marketing tactics that generates new customers the real deal estate agents and brokerages is Google Ads remarketing. A fairly new feature provided by remarketing is the capability to target people who recently visited specific websites and/or have typed in specific queries on Google. That way, you can easily target people who recently looked for "sell house," "buy house," or "Realtor" and people who visited multiple listing service (MLS) listings and real estate websites, including those of the competitors.

To create that targeting list, go to the Google Ads Campaign dashboard, create a remarketing list centered on interests, and add a list of website URLs and keywords. After this, your advertising banners will likely be served to people that are currently enthusiastic about buying or selling houses individuals who have visited these sites or searched for these keywords and certainly will drive qualified traffic in your region to your site.

Increase Your Network

Besides advertising on StreetEasy, Trulia, and Zillow and sending out monthly newsletters, my top strategy continues to be the personal touch. I host a monthly happy hour open bar in New York City and invite my top clients and their friends and families. It's a terrific way to increase your network organically, and I've gotten a number of my best sales clients that way. I strongly recommend it.

Target Serious Leads

One to generate leads system i love a whole lot is changing the message from "what's your home worth?" to "see exacltly what the home's selling price would be instantly when we put it on the market." This removes the lookie-loos who want to know very well what their investment is really worth so that you are more likely to get somebody wanting to sell and wants to know the price tag of the home. This will drive the prospect to an automated valuation model (AVM) lead capture landing page that could instantly provide them with what their asking price will be centered on active homes currently available on the market in their neighborhood.

Make your own Reference to Video Emails

It's an indisputable fact in 2019, video is king. Agents who are using video to promote their business are crushing it while those who don't are getting left within the dust. For those who have e-mail marketing campaigns set up but aren't converting leads, check out BombBomb that will help you create personalized videos, insert them to your marketing emails, and track engagement.

Host an Annual Party for Clients

As a Realtor, the answer to building a book of company is building relationships. To that end, our realty outfit always throws an annual Carvel ice cream gathering. The strategy is definitely a huge success as every year we build relationships with real people when you look at the neighborhood and also project our brand while making families happy with free ice cream. I could count several dozen deals we have closed through the years that directly flow from our annual frozen dessert extravaganza.

Harness the ability of Cold Calling

While there are many strategies [to real estate marketing], a recent trend has been the revival for the old marketing way of cold calling. New technology software has managed to make it easier than ever before for a genuine estate investor, agent, or broker to cold call with relative ease. For instance, a cloud-based service called Mojo Dialer will call three cell phone numbers at a time, allowing you to make 300 phone calls in an hour. It's also built to adhere to federal telemarketing rules so that you don't get fined.

Discovery has it that you can get about a 3% to 4% lead conversion rate [when cold-calling], so if you ensure it is a habit of calling for at the very least an hour or so each day, you may likely generate a few leads every day, which equates to sales on a regular basis. Buying lists and skip tracing [locating a person's whereabouts] the records for telephone numbers can cost between 25 cents to $1 per record depending on the services you use. So, if you spend $1,000 on generating an inventory, then diligently call the individuals regarding the list, you are likely to extract 30 to 40 leads and hopefully convert 1 or 2 of those leads into sales.

Use Strategic PR to construct Authority

While many agents think PR is one thing that only celebrities and titans of industry can afford, very few realize they can do it themselves — for free. Mike Fabbri uses sites like Help a Reporter Out (HARO) to pitch his expertise in real estate to journalists interested in sources. In exchange, he gets his name in the press plus the chance to get a link back once again to his website, that will be perfect for SEO.

Craft a Personalized Message for Your Buyers

I've found the most effective results come from an individual message within my voice. When you write your message, remember the following points:

Result in the message about them, They don't worry about you, so let them know how you can assist them to as soon as possible.

Be clear if a seller just isn't sure what you want them to complete, they'll never call you.

Suit your message to your seller

Make your message short and sweet In our fast-paced world, people rarely read all of their email; unsolicited mail often hits the trash can. If you prefer your message to be heard, allow it to be short.

Use Retargeting Campaigns to Drive Website Traffic

A robust method to strengthen your marketing is to set up retargeting campaigns. The concept is always to craft great ad copy that directs visitors to a dedicated landing page or a single-property website utilizing the listing you're marketing. The ad follows your site visitors across the internet and social media marketing, helping you redirect the traffic back once again to your internet site when they're readier to touch base.

Host Local Neighborhood Tours

With regards to great marketing, nothing beats the personal engagement which comes from hosting a fun event for the sphere. Even better why not host a meeting that shows off your personal love and expert knowledge about your farm area?

Luxury Manhattan real estate professional Jeff Goodman does exactly that. Goodman organizes regular walking tours of historic Manhattan neighborhoods for his sphere. Since he hires a professional tour guide when it comes to events, he generally gets 70 or more people to attend each tour.

Choose the Right Farm Area

Maximize the impact of these real estate marketing ideas by choosing the right farm area to establish yourself as a local expert and close more deals. To do so, research the typical age and income of local residents in addition to area amenities, and gain a comprehensive comprehension of your farm area's sales prices, turnover rate, and competition. When you select the right farm area, establish your presence with direct mailers, door hangers, and advertising.

Start an immediate Marketing Campaign

Postcards are an eye-catching and affordable solution to directly market to home buyers and homeowners in your farm area. You need to use direct mailers to market a nearby property to homeowners in a specific neighborhood, share statistics about recently sold properties, or promote your neighborhood real estate office.

Write a Killer Real Estate Newsletter

Once you opt to incorporate a drip email campaign into the real estate online strategy, create killer email newsletters. Relating to Outbound Engine, the subject line is the very first thing potential clients will discover, so use a powerful subject line to fully capture the eye of the readers. Email newsletters also needs to be according to a visually appealing template and include a call to action (CTA) that engages readers and converts leads into clients.

Create a New & Eye-catching Logo

Believe it or not, your logo the most important elements of your individual brand. A fantastic logo often helps propel you forward while a bad logo isn't going to help you attract more leads.

According to Patrick Sanders, creative director the real deal estate marketing powerhouse 1000watt, a great logo should "signal something exciting and new a note to your greater world that the organization is always changing and getting better. [Your work as an agent] should reflect that energy."

Master Your Elevator Pitch

Imagine you were given $5 million to market your business with a 30-second ad through the Super Bowl. What can you say? If this real question is causing you to be scratching your head, you need to work with your elevator pitch. A 30-second-or-less speech that shows off your specific skills and experience offers value and can end up producing more leads.

Use SEO to push Traffic to Your Website

SEO is a sensible way to use your business content to boost website visitors and expand the reach of one's marketing. Certain keywords like "houses for sale," "MLS," and "for sale by owner" or "FSBO" have higher SEO value than many other terms. Optimize your on line content much more with keywords which are extremely local, like "Prospect Heights townhouse," in the place of general keywords like "real estate on the market."

Create a Client Testimonial Packet

Client testimonials are a good solution to show potential home purchasers that you're well-established in your farm area. On its blog, idxcentral.com suggests ensuring you've got informative testimonials by asking clients targeted questions like, "What made you decide on me as your real estate professional?" Along with counting on clients to provide testimonials, touch base via SurveyMonkey or Yelp to solicit reviews. You should be certain to share positive testimonials via your site and social media.

Create Viral Infographics to fairly share on Social Media

Infographics take useful data and present them in an appealing and easy-to-read format. If you're on any Pinterest or Facebook real estate groups, you've likely seen and shared a large number of infographics already. At Fit Small Company, we use an instrument called Venngage to create great-looking infographics.

Share a Viral Real Estate Video

Videos that go viral via social media are nevertheless very popular. If you can capture someone's attention with a funny or insightful clip, it is possible to reach a wider audience through the effectiveness of social shares. Most people enjoy sharing entertaining videos on Twitter and with family. Regardless if the viewers isn't your target, they may send the video to a person who is.

The perfect real estate marketing ideas depend on your market, firm, and preferred lead management tools. Maximizing your online presence, sharing videos, and creating SEO-optimized content are effective tools for marketing your agency. Developing a marketing strategy also allows you to streamline to generate leads and client outreach so that you can concentrate on selling houses. Make sure to utilize the tips above to really make the much of your marketing efforts.

Some More Outside-the-Box Real Estate Marketing Ideas

Unique. Original. Remarkable. It's tough to develop real estate marketing ideas day in and day out that meet each of these criteria — especially once you spend a lot of your own time on the road meeting with clients and leads.

Sometimes, however, the best fix for marketing fatigue is thinking away from box and identifying ways your primary marketing channels – website, SEO, email marketing, paid advertising and social networking content – can differentiate your agency or brokerage through the competition. .

Below is, creative real estate marketing suggestions to help promote your agency and generate more leads. Whether you're just starting or are a professional realtor trying to attract new business, this guide will give you the tips and materials needed to build an effective marketing campaign.

Build a Rock Solid Marketing Foundation

The prosperity of your realtor industry relies on how well your internet marketing funnel attracts new house buyers. 44% of all of the home buyers and 99% of Millennials go to the Internet first when finding properties on the market. As a realtor, you need a professional website if you be prepared to increase revenue as time passes.

Home buyers expect quality while they search for homes therefore the realtor that best fits their demands. Your internet site should showcase your home listings, brand and expertise. Tools that help you stick out include:

- Branded messaging and images
- Responsive design
- IDX integration
- Blog content
- Lead capture landing pages
- Area pages

Your brand provides website visitors immediate understanding about who you really are, your expertise and how you're positioned to help them. A responsive realtor website means your pages show perfectly no real matter what type of device (desktop, laptop, tablet or cell phone) your prospects use when accessing your content.

Publish a nearby market quiz on the real estate website

In the event that you've ever checked out BuzzFeed before, then chances are you know people want to take quizzes on virtually any subject. Test your audience with a quick, multiple-choice quiz on something of great interest. See if they know things like which famous people was raised in the area and tidbits about your town's history. The questions or topics can even be created around broader subjects unrelated to your market, like music, movies, or some other element of pop culture.

If you want to function as the ultimate resource for your leads, however, a thought-provoking quiz regarding the ins and outs of selling or buying a home, such as the one below from Kevin Ho and Jonathan McNarry of San Francisco-based Vanguard Properties, could possibly be your ticket to gaining their confidence.

Think about these quick exams as you of the real estate marketing tools to make use of every now and then — perhaps as part of your marketing with email campaign. You might even create a contest round the quiz: Require people who take it to fill out a lead capture form by the end and give the winner something special card to a local restaurant or cafe.

Offer Home Valuations to Capture Seller Leads

Potential sellers need to know simply how much their home may be worth. Integrate a home valuation tool to your website and capture seller leads.

The following is a typical example of what this may seem like on your own site:

Valuation report

Once your visitor enters their address, they're prompted to deliver their current email address as well as other information so that you can view their home valuation report. After they provide this information, you've got an innovative new seller lead to contact.

Just because they will not sign up through email, you are able to follow-up through regular mail since your home valuation software has recently captured the home address.

Film an explainer video that goes into detail regarding the agency

Differentiate your business from other agents in your market with real estate explainer videos. Don a black turtleneck and explain your services as you were Steve Jobs (rest in peace). Pretend to be a political candidate and pitch people on why you're the right person to do the job. Heck, even take a full page out from the "Arrested Development" playbook and mock those awful 1-800 lawyer commercials.

These videos are traditionally meant to be serious, because they relay your value proposition and the thing that makes your agency successful and worth hiring. But as noted, personality plays a large role when you look at the decision-making of buyers and sellers, so have a blast while still getting across the info that's needed for consumers to know about your brand.

Provide a no cost moving truck

That is an original solution to get noticed in your local market. Invest in a moving truck along with your branding regarding the side. Offer it to your customers when they purchase or sell their property. Your online business benefits from additional branding and advertising each time your clients place the truck to make use of.

Get creative when clients don't need your moving truck. Go on it to home shows. Park it in elements of town that benefit you with high volumes of vehicle and pedestrian traffic.

Answer buyer/seller questions in your blog

An effective way to get ideas for blog content will be identify questions your target market is asking. Two tools assist you in finding these lists of questions:

- Answer The General Public
- People Also Ask

Answer The Public is a free tool that generates a summary of questions according to your keyword search. For instance, if you type in "los angeles homes", the questions received from this search can sometimes include:

- Must I buy a los angeles home?
- Simply how much will it be to get a los angeles home?

People Also Ask is a free feature inside a Google

search:

People also ask

A third tool for finding interesting searches to target is a chrome extension called Keywords Everywhere. It gives you related searches (along with estimated search volume) to any Google search:

Keywords Everywhere

Add some flavor to your real estate video marketing.

Sending a contact to your contacts to wish them a happy holiday likely won't nurture your leads through the sales funnel like blog posts and promotional email messages do. With that said, getting in the spirit for widely celebrated goings-on locally or nationally can humanize your brand.

Have a look at what the group at Modern Life Realty and ERA Justin Realty teams accomplished in listed here recordings: The former takes a normal video marketing technique and turns it on its head by talking to the camera with ... well ... whatever it is the featured gentleman is donning. Meanwhile, the latter hops on the "Call Me Maybe" bandwagon (which has long since been abandoned, but that is another story) and capitalizes on its fifteen minutes of fame.

Both took a chance, that is that which you have to do from time to time together with your real estate online strategy, as these tactics can often pay big dividends.

Together with these outlandish videos, consider conducting "man-on-the-street" interviews as well. The subjects of the videos don't need certainly to pertain to your business if not real estate as a whole. You could question them philosophical questions, like what this is of life is, or inquire further for his or her thoughts on an area college or professional sports team.

Develop a blog post or video series highlighting great area restaurants and entertainment.

Though property price, size, style, and features will be the top considerations for the modern home buyer, residing in a residential district with plentiful food and entertainment options is an ever more important aspect as well.

Yelp, TripAdvisor, and a wealth of other websites offer up reviews and facts about movie theaters, restaurants, and similar businesses. However these portals have an issue: they are able to take forever to sort through merely to find a well-written review or locate the best information. That's for which you, the all-knowing real estate professional, comes into play.

Develop a number of blog posts and/or videos that provides home buyers interested in your market the lowdown on the premier eateries and establishments in your area.

Finding these locales shouldn't be a challenge simply think of your own favorite places to see a play or grab a bite with friends. Then, jot down why you adore those places and share your opinions utilizing the world, like Realtor Michelle Calkins does in her blog post series and Realtor David Gonzalez does into the YouTube clip.

Order unique business cards that stick out.

Business cards will never walk out style. You'll also have in-person meetings and meet-ups with buyers, sellers, and other industry professionals, meaning it is vital to have your information readily available to generally share using them. But a boring card that lists your online business name and contact information when you look at the smallest, plainest font won't be memorable.

Take a risk and order some original business cards few have likely seen before. For example, take a good look at these fine examples featured on ViralNova that use the concept to the next level.

Research the best business card creation services on the market and attempt to find one that proposes to develop distinct versions like the one above that will get individuals to remember you long after your conversation with them ends. It may seem like a little item to target so much of your attention on, but marketing for real estate agents will continue to evolve and start to become more competitive because of the day, so seemingly minor touches such as this are able to keep you top-of-mind.

Incorporate your furry friend into several of your real estate listing photos.

Though its not all home buyer will take care of seeing a cute French bulldog or Grumpy Cat look-alike throughout a property they tour on your own real estate website, chances are the occasional photo featuring pets won't turn fully off consumers and may even appeal to your buyers you're interested in.

Use your pup or cat, or borrow one from a family member or friend, to feature in your listing shots. (Side note: If you somehow convince your canine pal to have in the relaxed pose due to the fact one above, as featured in this Curbed article, you really need to take up a side business as your dog whisperer).

Use Instagram Stories

The answer to building your brand on Instagram (and all sorts of social networking platforms) is to become great at getting your followers to engage to you. Instagram Stories provide you with an approach for generating engagement and gaining brand recognition in the act.

One method to use Instagram Stories is always to run a giveaway or contest. Direct followers to take screenshots while they listen directly into your IG Live segment and direct message you those images. Choose a winner and present them something fun or helpful (a free book about qualifying for a financial loan, for instance).

Cross pollinate your social networking channels using the above method. Utilize it together with your Facebook Lives or tweets to get your FB and Twitter followers to realize you on Instagram.

Devise a fun game to accompany awards shows or televised events

Ever see publications, bloggers, and brands share "drinking games" for events like the Academy Awards additionally the Super Bowl? Participate in and produce your own personal form of a casino game (of this drinking variety or something different is your decision). You can even create an interactive or printable bingo chart, of sorts, (see The Wall Street Journal's interactive take below) for people to make use of during these events to check out in case the amusing insights and predictions come true. Brand this marketing collateral along with your logo to get those who partake in your game to remember where they first got it.

Post ideas and strategies for homeowners, buyers, and sellers in Reddit.

Before you can get all flustered wondering how Reddit will help your real estate marketing (or what Reddit even is), just know that the website isn't simply the "front page of the internet," as it promotes itself to be. You will find endless quantities of "subreddit" forum boards on the website dedicated to the essential specific topics on the planet including homeownership, home buying, and home selling. Find ones by which people looking to purchase or sell properties need sage wisdom and where homeowners are searching for advice regarding their mortgages or tax tips.

Capitalize on the rise in popularity of the latest internet memes.

You may be thinking memes are simply another internet distraction — one that keeps you against completing important tasks, like segmenting real estate leads in your customer relationship management (CRM) database or scheduling meetings with prospective clients. On the contrary, though: Memes offer a (dare we say) fun real estate marketing tactic that is at the moment taking off with agents and certainly will get some laughs from your own audience.

The next you observe that a (politically correct and totally appropriate-for-work) meme is making the rounds online, try to come up with ways to use it on Facebook, Twitter, Instagram, or Pinterest (like Realtor Paul Fernandez's board above), and even on your blog. A post titled "10 Feelings All Home

Buyers Have throughout the Process" filled with memes could be your key to connecting with your targeted demographic.

Fabricate mock logos for your agency that replicate famous ones.

If you're a large fan of a specific television show, incorporate the famous typeface and/or imagery connected with one (or maybe more) of this series with your personal real estate logo. Make it timely by sharing a message with your list featuring your new, short-term branding and an email about when the new season premieres. There are many directions you can take this faux-go (have it?), so find a well-known pop culture design or symbol you can mess around with for your own real estate marketing. Just be sure not to ever utilize it in too many promotional materials (the very last thing you would like is to find a cease-and-desist from billion-dollar entities).

Send Handwritten Notes

You have the opportunity to offer your prospects and clients a unique experience once they open a mailed envelope and discover a handwritten note inside.

Combine this strategy with all the home valuation tool mentioned previously. Send handwritten notes to your home valuation leads that failed to enter their email address.

Create a referral system

While you create your online presence and leadflow, don't forget about getting referrals from happy clients. One of the easiest ways to get referrals would be to simply ask. Concentrate on providing your prospects a smooth transition for the entire real estate process and then inquire further who they know.

Staying dedicated to providing ongoing tips and helpful content to email subscribers will foster more referrals. Send periodic content to your clients providing you with house owner tips. This high touch follow-up keeps you "top of mind" when past customers hear that friends and family are looking to buy a house.

Real Estate Marketing Niches

- Real Estate Branding Ideas
- Real Estate SEO Tips
- Real Estate Advertisement Ideas
- Real Estate Social Media Ideas

- Real Estate Listing Marketing Ideas
- Real Estate Email Ideas
- Real Estate Social Video Marketing Ideas
- Offline Real Estate Marketing Ideas

Real Estate Branding Ideas

Develop a solid real estate agent bio and add it to your About Page.

When leads find your brand online, they must be able to get a powerful sense of your professional qualifications and personality. Craft a real estate bio that leads will cherish, detailing your experiences, values, and interests, and place it prominently on the 'About Me' page of one's website.

You may be your brand, which means that your personal photograph should exude an amiable demeanor and elevate your brand with an expert look.

Hire a specialist photographer who is able to provide advice on positioning, and who is able to ensure that the final product is crisp and presentable in many different formats. If you're low on funds at the beginning of your job, you can even choose to take one all on your own that looks professional.

Develop a value proposition.

Should you want to be a fruitful agent, you must not have only unique characteristics that set you apart through the competition, you should certainly define what those unique features mean to your clients, leads, and community.

A quick value proposition should exhibit your value and strengths as a representative. This statement are going to be reused in your marketing materials over and over again.

Prepare a 30-second pitch to use when talking to new leads.

If you created a value proposition (above), you are able to think about a pitch as something very similar. But how things are keep reading paper doesn't necessarily translate well to personal interactions.

In your initial conversations with leads, you need to be capable of making a quick but powerful statement that conveys you're a knowledgeable agent that knows the market better than anyone. Once you've created your pitch, practice it out loud.

Acquire some swag printed with your branding.

Brand exposure in your town might help increase your business. Get items like calendars, pens, keychains, and notepads, and have now your name, logo, and email address printed on them to pass off to clients or at local events.

A company's online star rating is the no. 1 factor used by consumers to evaluate a company.

Online reviews have a prominent presence in search engines, have a sizable effect on your business's reputation, and tend to be an important source of lead referrals. Seize control of the brand by requesting online reviews from good past clients, and then make it easy in order for them to post in multiple places.

Ask your best former clients for testimonials.

Happy past clients are your best brand ambassadors. Their opinions and feedback on your own site will give your brand social clout. Approach a few of your very best former clients and get if they would offer feedback for a testimonial. Written is good, but testimonials with photos or video are even better.

Have an original signature item or look.

Many agents have an exceptional look, whether it's a color they wear often, a method of dress, a hat, or hairstyle (our VP of Marketing, Seth Price is known for his pink-hued pants). Develop a confident, distinctive factor for the personal brand this is certainly recognizable and memorable.

Set up squeeze pages or lead capture forms on your own site for lead gen.

Lead capture forms are excellent how to secure lead information to help you take communication into the hands. Put up squeeze pages after someone clicks on a residential property advertisement, or maybe before someone gets all the information about a residential property on the site.

Additionally, it's also wise to have optional lead capture forms on each website page for leads thinking about getting more information. Forms should ask for name, phone number, email, and also a location where someone can pose a question.

Place your contact information on every page of your website.

With to generate leads being one of your top priorities, your contact information shouldn't be hidden or only using one page of your website. Prominently showcase your contact info on every page to make it easy for contributes to reach out.

Include beautiful royalty-free local imagery.

With regards to building a good online experience for the website visitors, nothing does the work quite in addition to local photography. Getting usage of royalty-free images could be difficult, but use one of the numerous online and local resources to get great shots of the local area.

Give leads expense information and calculators.

Most clients have financial questions. Create a document you are able to share with leads to assist them to calculate their expenses, before, during, and after a sale.

Use calls to action to boost user engagement.

Many people place calls to action at the end of a blog post, you should make use of them various other regions of your internet site as well:

- sidebar prompts to sign up for your newsletters

- a homepage area asking folks to get in touch with you
- or near the top of lead capture forms so folks could possibly get more information on a residential property

Effective calls to action include enticing copy that get a person to do this on the site.

Add testimonials to your homepage.

When you've requested testimonials from your happiest and most vocal clients, showcase them on your homepage to leverage the social proof they provide.

Add social sharing buttons to your site.

Social sharing is a massive section of generating referral traffic and building brand recognition online. This procedure should always be possible for your website visitors so everyone can click them and share your articles quickly with reduced effort. Many website themes carry these as standard, or you can choose to install a plugin for the site.

Write and publish content on the blog regularly.

Successful inbound marketing starts with consistent content creation. This enhances your quest engine optimization, generates traffic, and provides real value to your customers.

Consistency is crucial in blogging: You should be prepared to publish between 2–5 blog posts each week on your own market, listings, area details, and real estate statistics. See these 101 blog post ideas for inspiration.

Develop guides for buyers and sellers.

Just about any lead you encounter will probably have a lot of questions regarding buying or selling, which means you're probably answering similar questions over repeatedly and scrambling to find resources that can help them.

Make your own downloadable or printable guides you can easily give to leads such as lots of information on processes and expectations.

Vary post types.

Not every bit of content has got to be a long-form piece. In fact, most readers love variety. Create a mix of written blogs, ebooks, infographics, videos, photos, lists, etc.

Curate content from other sources to incorporate on your own site.

Its not all bit of content on the site has to be completely original. Effectively curating content from other sites, crediting the first source, and adding your very own perspective makes content creation simple and quick.

Use analytics to operate a vehicle your marketing.

Whether it's a bit of content that gets high traffic, a listing that gets high time-on-site statistics, or an influx in referrals from a specific blogger, monitor your site analytics and visitor behavior to ascertain where you should focus your marketing.

Real Estate Listing Marketing Ideas

Optimize listing pages.

Optimize your listing pages with local keywords, proper address formatting, and appropriately sized photos, in addition to necessary links.

Feature top listings from the home page

Your house page is normally one of the most visited pages in your website. Make the most of this traffic by offering your best listings here.

Construct great real estate listing copy.

Great writing could make or break a listing's potential. The smallest amount details won't do the trick if you would like have the best leads while offering. Write great real estate listing copy with interesting adjectives and descriptions that entice readers.

Make your listings look their best.

Stage properties and hire a professional photographer to fully capture the very best angles of every room.

Dedicate blog posts or landing pages to showcase your listings at length.

A dedicated post or landing page for a list makes it possible to build a robust marketing campaign for a property (beyond just the listing page).

Add more in-depth descriptions, photos, video, and information on the area to higher pitch the property. So that you can attract organic traffic, optimize the post with:

- hyper-local keywords

- address names
- and property type keywords

Share the blog along with your network while you would an everyday blog post.

Advertise listings in a separate newsletter to your leads and clients.

Leverage email's great ROI by making use of your newsletter to advertise your listings to clients. Keep your message fairly brief and to-the-point, adding in alluring subject lines and headers, a few striking photos, descriptive detail, and a hyperlink to your listing or website landing page when it comes to property.

Create video presentations for your listings.

Photos are anticipated included in listings, but video can build a fuller experience for the leads and provide them a more in-depth perspective in the property. Create professional property videos for priority listings to generate a host of great interest.

Post listing all about every social networking outlet.

Listings on your own website are great, but let your followers know about new featured listings by posting them on each social media site.

Develop listing boards on Pinterest.

Pinterest is a great platform to create mood or informational boards around listings.

Include pictures of your property, scenes and highlights regarding the area, and general advice and tips for buyers. Make sure to include your contact information and links into the listing page or squeeze page for the listing.

Real Estate Social Media Marketing Ideas

Social media marketing

Your brand must have a stronger presence on social media, as they are a significant driver of successful marketing campaigns and referral traffic.

Even although you don't currently use all of them, it's good practice to secure usernames on every platform just in case you choose to use them later, including Facebook, Twitter, Google+, LinkedIn, Pinterest, YouTube, SlideShare, Foursquare and Instagram. If possible, make use of the same account name across all platforms.

Create custom social media bios for every single platform.

Every social media site is unique: Their users interact differently and expect different sorts of personality (think a hilarious video on Facebook versus a vocation advice article on LinkedIn).

Additionally, each platform provides you with different amounts of space to publish a bio. Write social networking bios that be noticeable on each platform but still sound consistent across all of your social media marketing channels.

Invite relatives and buddies to such as your pages or follow you.

Every page starts with zero, so let your personal network to offer your web social brands a boost.

Invite friends, family, colleagues, and past clients to like or follow your professional pages so you can build an instantaneous following (and they also can easily see and share what you post).

Add social media retargeting tags to your internet site

As you understand that most people to your site won't convert to customers immediately, it's important to utilize retargeting. And also this applies to email leads who don't convert straight away.

Retargeting is a way for which you place an item of code, called a pixel, on the website pages. This then allows you to "retarget", or "remarket" to those people across different social networking platforms.

As an example, a Facebook pixel on your own site allows you to place an ad in the front of these visitors the very next time each goes on Facebook. Can be done the same along with other channels like Twitter, YouTube, Instagram and LinkedIn.

This marketing method lets you re-engage prospects no matter where they're going. It builds your brand and creates awareness regarding the services every time a past site visitor sees your offerings.

Post regularly on each social media marketing platform.

Social media marketing is only as potent as how it is used.

Successful agents using social media know it requires a regular posting to build an audience that may engage with you. This means posting just about every day on your core social media sites.

Use our post to find out more in what types of content work best on each social site.

Include social follow buttons on your own website.

You should ensure it is more than easy for folks to get and follow your social media accounts. Whether or not it's in your header, footer, or sidebar, ensure your icons are prominent on the page.

Showcase your savvy with video.

Video specials that offer your real estate knowledge, advice to buyers and sellers, or give in-depth previews of listings can deliver a significant return in your marketing.

Additionally, optimizing your YouTube videos can boost the SEO of the content.

Get a social media scheduler.

Being an enthusiastic poster on social media marketing doesn't have to mean being glued to your computer or laptop every minute of the day. Many posts, like blog posts, announcements, property details, and general advice could be scheduled in advance using automated systems like Hootsuite, Buffer, or Edgar.

Generate slideshows.

Multimedia presentations made out of content on your own website can build readership from audiences who prefer visuals to plain text. Publishing slideshows on platforms like SlideShare puts your articles right in front of potentially tens and thousands of users.

Join a Twitter discussion

Twitter is a superb platform to activate with other professionals or leads. Follow major real estate related topics by searching relevant hashtags and offer thoughts or pose questions.

You may host your own personal Twitter chat, in which case you'll need to advertise it to your leads via email and social networking, allowing them to know how to engage with you through that time and energy to get their questions answered.

Develop or join groups, and begin discussions there to create thought leadership.

Many discussions and coalitions are made within

social media groups. Join some to create your network, or create your own to build a resource where you are able to offer advice.

Run a contest through social networking.

Contests may be a good way to come up with leads. Use social networking to host a contest, and gives a prize, like a present card to an area business or a free of charge consultation.

Publish new, original thoughtful articles on LinkedIn.

LinkedIn now allows one to create thoughtful articles inside their publisher platform. Applying this platform can get your ideas right in front of a huge number of readers.

Real Estate Advertisement Ideas

Discover ways to set up advertising campaigns.

Whether it's for search engines or social media, learn the basics of setting goals, understanding pricing, and setting up campaigns.

Set your targets for the focused keywords you need to target additionally the types of customers who does result in the most qualified leads. You'll use this information later when setting up campaigns.

Whilst the length and scope of the copy depends on platform, most ads contain a value proposition and proactive approach. Write these early and present yourself a few choices to test against one another.

Choose a vendor to setup campaigns for you.

Setting up, monitoring, and tracking promotional initiatives needs time to work and lots of advertising savvy.

Agents who want to maximize the impact of these ads should make use of an established company where they are able to have a person oversee their campaigns and supply guidance on how they've been performing.

Creating an ad budget.

Understand the factors which will impact the investment you need to make to get the return you're hoping for. Then, calculate your PPC ROI predicated on your budget.

Use social media marketing.

Social media marketing advertising can place your message in the front of targeted users. Major networks like Facebook, Twitter, Google+, and LinkedIn offer choices to place your message in front of these large audiences.

Develop captivating graphics for ads.

The strongest ads have visual elements to attract users in. Create custom photos or video to pair along with your ads and maximize their potential.

Advertise in high-audience newsletters.

There are popular consumer-facing real estate brands that send out regular newsletters. Advertising there can place your ad in front of a large number of readers, but it's far better go with hyper-local newsletters.

Create a dedicated splash page attached to your ad.

Should you want to increase to generate leads from your ad, a click should lead to a website landing page in which you provide more worthiness to your lead (based on the content associated with the original ad), as well as a lead capture form.

Create custom media around featured properties.

For featured listings, create custom images, graphics, and video to promote the most effective components of a certain property.

Targeted video advertising of single properties.

Target specific users with YouTube advertising by showcasing captivating video of single properties.

Layer on retargeting across key channels

Identify the social media marketing channels most critical to your online business and re-engage your warm audience. For instance, target non-converting website visitors the very next time they visit Facebook, LinkedIn, Twitter or Instagram.

Real Estate SEO

Put up a Google My Business page

Google My Business lets you manage and control how your real estate industry appears in Google Search and Maps listings.

Filling out your NAP (name, address and phone

number) profile completely can help you show up properly in Google's 3-pack map listing:

LA RE agents

The main reason you want your agency to exhibit up in the 3-pack is simply because searchers pay attention to the visual aspect of the:

- map
- ratings
- prominent website and directions links
- the decision button on mobile devices

Getting your site placed in this top 3 listing area improves your possibilities to attract quality local leads.

Submit site to major aggregators

Most of the data spread throughout the neighborhood search ecosystem is handled because of the major data aggregators. Localeze, Factual, Acxiom and Infogroup would be the four major aggregators that publish local business information to social media, search engines, directories and review websites.

Submitting your details to these aggregators increases your chances that Google as well as other search engines take your business seriously. You certainly will gain an aggressive advantage when you've listed your agency correctly, while other local real estate professionals and brokers have neglected to do this.

Ensure consistent NAP across all online properties

Employ a consistent approach when filling out company information during the major aggregators or directories. A large part to upping your local search engine rankings would be to make sure that every listing is consistent with the second.

As an example, each listing needs to have your organization name, address, contact number and website listed a similar. This prevents duplicate listings and avoids confusion as internet search engine algorithms regulate how to rank your company.

More specifically, any online property that lists your NAP is named a citation. Google and Bing consider NAP inconsistencies across citations as an adverse search signal. Should your business has 3 similar listings inside one directory, for instance, the search engines don't know which one is accurate.

This creates doubt in the algorithm regarding how trustworthy the company is. The end result is a diminished search ranking.

When you consider that Google's search market share is close to 90%, you want to be sure you do everything possible to increase your presence there:

Set up schema

Schema enables you to mark up elements in your site in a manner that helps Google determine what the data means. Through schema markups, you will get the ability to tell Google just how to attractively present your information.

For example, take a look at how you can list your upcoming open house directly into the search results and inquire yourself about the quality of leadflow that results from this marketing method:

Conduct key word research

Your real estate advertising campaign should include a thorough policy for taking advantage of keyword searches employed by future site visitors. You can find 3 basic kinds of real estate keywords to research and employ:

- Primary (ex, newport beach homes)

- Secondary (ex, orange county real estate)
- Long-tail (ex, tips for buying real estate in costa mesa)

These areas are further segmented with regards to:

- buyer intent (realtor near me, santa ana houses on the market, etc)
- sort of sale (luxury vs foreclosure)
- property type (house vs condo)
- location (oceanfront vs lake)
- Information gathering stage (do I need a realtor, house buying tips, etc)

Of course, you want to attract qualified prospects thinking of buying now. Don't underestimate the effectiveness of attracting site leads that are when you look at the information gathering stage, however. Warm these prospects up, get them to trust you and then benefit once they decide this is the time to start out thinking of buying their next bit of real estate.

Several tools exist to assist you research your following set of real estate keywords:

- Ahrefs (paid tool)
- ahrefs

- Ubersuggest (free tool)
- ubersuggest Re
- Answer the general public (free tool)
- answerpublicRE

Build local landing pages

A proper estate squeeze page is a single page on your site which allows you to talk with a particular segment of your target audience.

For example, if you're targeting a keyword such as for example "guide to buying Phoenix real estate", you'll get much more leads pointing your visitors to a landing page offering a free guide for purchasing real estate in Phoenix than pointing them to a generic home page.

Since multiple landing pages causes a 120% rise in leadflow, it is important to master how to make use of the various real estate splash page methods.

Collect reviews on major 3rd party review sites

There was a primary correlation amongst the amount of reviews your agency collects and the local search engine rankings. In fact, ranking signals account fully for 15.44% of Google's local search rankings:

Local search factors

Your interaction with reviews is vital. Google states specifically to their Google My Business help page which they not only pay attention to reviews that are positive in terms of ranking sites, but that your particular interaction with reviewers is a factor.

Build local backlinks

Increasing the number of other sites linking to your real estate website will enhance your search engine rankings:

Monitor backlinks

The cause of it is that more incoming links to your internet site improves your domain authority and so, overall keyword rankings across your entire site.

Real Estate Email Marketing Ideas

Create an email signature with essential details.

Your email signature should include your complete name, phone number, email address, and website address that links straight to your internet site. Not just is this an easy way to produce your information, it means that in case your email is forwarded, the recipient will discover all your brand details as well.

Put up email sign-up forms in your site to cultivate your recipient list.

You can only get a good return on your investment in email when you yourself have a considerable recipient list. Use on-site sign-up forms with effective calls to action to have readers to join up.

Put up autoresponders for thank-yous if not immediately available.

Whether it's late during the night or you're away at a conference, set up autoresponder messages to let clients and leads know you're not immediately available but that you'll get back into them at the earliest opportunity.

The exact same goes for messages to those who download a reference from your own site or RSVP to an event.

Construct responsive email templates that look good on every device.

Email templates also come in all sizes and

shapes, you ought to be using a newsletter template with responsive design and clean layout.

Segment your email list.

If you would like give very personal experiences to your leads, segment your email list predicated on client personas and needs. Then, target communications with details pertinent to each client.

Personalize emails.

Including a recipient's name as well as other details from your interactions can make emails feel more personal and certainly will deepen their trust.

Use storytelling and imagery to boost engagement.

Include effective storytelling elements and videos or images to increase click-through and conversion rates for the emails.

Add social media accounts and share buttons to your emails.

Increase cross-platform engagement by encouraging users to fairly share your email content right on their social media marketing accounts with share buttons put into your email. Use a modern template to obtain these features.

Adapt your email calls to action according to needs.

Make use of your list segmentation and lead tracking to figure out the very best proactive approach to supply each lead as a next thing, whether that's getting new contributes to subscribe to your newsletter or getting a client close to sale to download a closing checklist.

Develop a message course for leads.

Your leads are most likely facing similar roadblocks or questions. Increase email engagement by offering an exclusive email course to go over various real estate issues, offering a fresh tip each day or week.

Offline Real Estate Marketing Ideas

Establish partnerships with geographic area businesses.

Develop relationships with local businesses and ask for to place your real estate cards or listing information at their desk or bulletin board.

Sponsor local events.

Local events, churches, schools, and sports events are constantly seeking sponsors. Look into fees in return for brand advertising on booklets, t-shirts, banners, flyers, etc.

Host free seminars on topics concerning buyers or sellers in your area.

Don't just offer value to locals when you have a list in the marketplace. Find areas to host informal sessions to offer your knowledge and advice to locals. Use a sign-in sheet to get information so you can follow up with attendees after.

Advertise your company and listings in local media.

Advertise your brand in local media like newspapers, magazines, radio, television, etc. To have your messaging right in front of local leads.

Take local sponsorships one step further.

Be creative with local sponsorship opportunities: Sponsor the coffee mugs at your local coffee shop, the golf tee boxes at a golf club, or a stand at the local farmers market.

Run an open house.

Develop open houses where you could interact closely with local leads and offer intimate walk-throughs.

Make sure the house is staged well, and offer a lot of snacks, packets in regards to the property, and free swag together with your company logo. Collect information via an open house sign-in sheet and follow through with leads a single day after your event.

Use custom banners, balloons, and signs to market your open house.

Build brand recognition every time you host an open house by providing signage and other extras. Go the additional mile by putting your name brand or logo to them.

Create a physical high-quality mailer.

Mailers might help get listings and your brand in the possession of of everyone in your community. Use high-gloss paper and sophisticated design to build premier real estate mailers for your area.

Write a consistent column for the local media.

A consistent column in your neighborhood

newspaper, magazine, or online blog will help you present your knowledge to an area audience and build recognition in your community. If you're a much better talker, add your thoughts to a regular radio show.

Attend local events and join local meetup groups and associations.

Being a force in the local community means turning up in places where you can build real face-to-face relationships. Use local groups, festivals, or meetings to develop your contact base.

Real Estate Video Promotion Tips and Ideas

Interview happy customers

Person to person recommendations are a powerful method to help prospects understand your value. Take care to interview past customers and permit their words to accomplish the heavy lifting with regards to pointing out of the features of working with you specifically.

Don't forget to enhance your interviews beyond past clients. Interview home inspectors, mortgage brokers, construction company owners along with other people you work with through the entire entire procedure of a house sale.

It's your possibility to show your prospects the positive way everyone you work with looks upon you.

Shoot video tours of most listings

Showing is obviously a lot better than telling. Using listing videos to showcase the properties you have got on the market is one of the most effective how to help prospects see precisely what each property offers them.

This will be a method to get prospects motivated to raise their relationship with you and schedule phone and in-person meetings.

Publish home/buyer educational videos

Educational videos that offer real estate buyers advice are an approach to establish credibility. It is a real estate marketing idea that reveals your expertise and shows prospects exactly how much you're interested in educating them regarding the advantages and pitfalls involved in their purchase decisions.

Focus in on mortgage options, how to save for an advance payment, tax advantages to owning a property, the necessity of inspection reports and other similar topics you know your buyers will benefit from learning about.

Record neighborhood community videos

Create videos that showcase the area and community atmosphere across the homes you sell. Your prospects wish to know they're moving into a safe area with excellent schools, parks and surrounding neighborhoods.

Showcase other homes, businesses, developments, restaurants, shopping areas and other neighborhood features that help your buyers determine what variety of community they're potentially stepping into.

Promote helpful how-to videos

Use helpful "how-to" video content to instruct prospects step-by-step methods to solve challenges or realize important concepts you know they ought to understand throughout the buying experience.

For example, a how-to video that walks a prospect through the method for selecting their realtor goes quite a distance in getting them to see you since the perfect choice.

Add videos to email drip series

Don't forget to include your video content within your email follow-up sequences. Create a welcome drip series so that new subscribers receive videos with your written content.

Promote videos across social media channels

It's important to combine your entire social media platforms into one synergistic real estate advertising campaign. Prevent the tendency to produce videos and use YouTube since the only distribution channel.

Instead, take that content and distribute across Facebook, Instagram, Twitter and any kind of social channel you determine to use as part of your marketing efforts.

How to Build a fruitful Real Estate Marketing Campaign

Set clear goals

Identify which objectives you'll strive to achieve. Create a strategy and understand what types of habits you will need to grow into.

Are you going to assess the wide range of sales each month? What number of new leads generated every month? Think about which marketing strategy shall help you accomplish each goal.

Use activity goals, too. For example, hone in on a particular quantity of calls in order to make each day. You'll experience pros and cons when marketing your real estate business. Measuring activity helps ensure that you'll continue spending so much time when results haven't shown themselves yet.

Identify your target customer

Marketing always is best suited when its messaging is focused on a certain segment of the overall market. As an example, your marketing will need to speak one method to investors and an entirely different way in the event your target customers are very first time home buyers.

Establish your unique selling proposition

Figuring out your unique selling proposition (USP) identifies how exactly to set yourself aside from other real estate professionals.

Think about the thing that makes you unique. What would you bring towards the table that they don't?

Can it be your experience?

Your personality?

Your knowledge of this area?

Or something else?

How does your USP provide value to your customers and encourage them to work well with you?

Choose marketing channels to reach audience

Decide which marketing channels to use. It's impractical to discover the time for you to use every social media platform available and optimize each channel effectively. Choose where your time and effort will undoubtedly be used best.

Are you going to use an online site? Are you going to blog often? Will you use Facebook, Twitter, YouTube or other social networking option? Find the marketing channels which make the most sense according to your personality as well as other skill-sets.

Define a lead nurturing strategy

Heat up email leads by periodically sending them information that builds trust and reveals your expertise. Send out new blog posts to your newsletter list. Provide your subscribers with neighborhood updates, housing market trends, how-to videos, details about simple tips to qualify for that loan, walk-through videos of the latest listings, etc.

Select tools to make usage of the plan

Make a listing of the tools had a need to put your real estate marketing campaign into action. Determine your email service provider, project management software, event software, website creation software as well as other brand building tools.

Measure performance

Define precise metrics to measure achievement with. Use goals that easily inform you whether you've strike the mark within specific timeframes.

Don't write, "I will increase my lead flow".

Instead, create a goal that says, "I will generate 500 new email subscribers into the month of June." You will be aware for sure at the conclusion of the month whether 500 new leads were generated or perhaps not.

Ready. Set. Market.

As you care able to see, there are lots of ways to market your real estate business.

Invest some time to determine which strategies take advantage sense for you personally and then create your foundation. Focus on the steps that build off of assets you have in place. For example, if you have got a large Facebook following already, try to find tips above that help you maximize that audience.

Then, transfer to other areas that logically build your web site larger. It's very easy to become overwhelmed. The important thing is always to plan out the long-term strategy and then start implementing that plan step-by-step each week.

Finally, make certain your entire real estate strategies revolve around your site. Your site will be your "home" on the net. It's the place where most lead flow and business will come from.

Create your brand. Increase your traffic. Enjoy a steady upsurge in revenue from your own real estate business.

Real Estate Terms to Know

Having a simple knowledge of important real estate concepts prior to starting the homebuying process will provide you with peace of mind now and may help save you a lot of money in the future. Check out real estate terms you should know before you begin trying to find a home. In the event that you still have questions or will be ready to start touring homes, a Redfin real estate professional will be very happy to help.

Buyer's Agent vs. Listing Agent

You will find usually two agents involved once you buy a property; the "buyer's agent," who represents you, therefore the "listing agent," who represents the home seller. Dual agency occurs when there is certainly only 1 agent representing both sides of this transaction, and it's also something you wish to avoid without exceptions!

Fixed Rate vs. Adjustable Rate Mortgages

Conventional loans include "fixed rate" and "adjustable rate" mortgages. A hard and fast rate mortgage has a predetermined rate of interest for the lifetime of the mortgage; the most typical are for 30 years. A variable rate mortgage has a variable interest rate; the most frequent are for 5, 7, or ten years.

Pre-approval Letter

Before you make an application for a mortgage if not start looking for a home, you ought to get a pre-approval letter through the bank, that will be an estimate of just how much they'll lend you. This letter will help you know what you can afford, and ensures home sellers you will be able to get that loan when needed.

Listings

Real estate professionals frequently make reference to homes for sale as "listings." A "listing" on an internet site shows information on the home, like the price and number of bedrooms.

Inspection

After you've made an offer on a home, you'll need to schedule an inspection, which costs around $500 – $800, with regards to the market. The inspector will go through every nook and cranny, and review things such as the plumbing, electrical, foundation, walls, heating, and appliances.

Appraisal

When you apply for a mortgage, your lender will need an appraisal of the property you wish to buy. A licensed appraiser will estimate the home's value centered on comparable homes which have sold in your community and an investigation for the property.

Contingencies

Once you place in an offer on a house, you can specify certain problems that must certanly be met ahead of the deal will go through they are called contingencies. You have to ensure you can actually obtain the loan (a financing contingency), that the inspection does not show anything too crazy (inspection contingency), and that the appraised value is close to what you're offering to cover (appraisal contingency). Those are only several common examples; there are numerous other forms of contingencies, that you should consult with your agent.

Offers and Contracts

Once you find the appropriate home, you'll make an offer from the property with the aid of an agent or attorney. If the seller counters your original offer, it is usually simply because they want additional money or a faster timeline for closing the offer, from which point you'll need to negotiate. When submitting an offer, it is smart to add an individual touch by including a cover letter which explains why you want to purchase the home.

Closing Costs

Be prepared to pay plenty of fees whenever you purchase a house. Typically, closing costs will amount to 2-5% associated with purchase price of your home, and therefore doesn't through the down payment. Common fees include excise tax, loan-processing costs and title insurance.

Title Insurance

After all of the negotiations are done while the seller has accepted your offer, you need to receive a property title report within per week. Most mortgage lenders require you to pay title insurance within the closing costs; title insurers search the general public records to make sure the house seller actually had rights to your title and that there aren't any liens in the home (like an unpaid contractor or unpaid taxes).

ABOUT THE AUTHOR

Diego De Giovanni is a real estate expert, an Italian national specifically from Turin. He kicked off his real estate marketing career in the year 1999 starting with local landscape. Years after properly understanding the principles needed to succeed in the local landscape sector of real estate, he began his passionate exploration of the residential market.

Having conquered both local landscape and residential market for 10 years, he began exploring the opportunities in the London market which gave him the opportunity to collaborate with a real estate company specializing in residential trading. Back in Itay, he has helped several real estate companies start, and nurture their businesses to success.

In the meantime he decides to study the American real estate market to better understand it's dynamics and does so through a big in the industry.

His success did not end with the achievement he has made in Italy, helping businesses. He went further to achieve a path to becoming a Mental Coach while specializing in business and assisting them get result.